11 rg

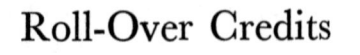

Roll-Over Credits

By the same author

The Case Against Floating Exchanges

The Case Against Joining the Common Market

Decline and Fall? Britain's Crisis in the Sixties

The Destiny of the Dollar

The Destiny of Gold

A Dynamic Theory of Forward Exchange

The Euro-Bond Market

The Euro-Dollar System: Practice and
Theory of International Interest Rates

Foreign Exchange Crises

The History of Foreign Exchange

Leads and Lags: The Main Cause of Devaluation

Parallel Money Markets
(two volumes)

A Textbook on Foreign Exchange

A Textbook on Monetary Policy

ROLL-OVER CREDITS

The System of Adaptable Interest Rates

by

PAUL EINZIG

Macmillan

© Paul Einzig 1973

All rights reserved. No part of this publication may be
reproduced or transmitted, in any form or by any
means, without permission.

First published 1973 by
THE MACMILLAN PRESS LTD
London and Basingstoke

*Associated companies in New York
Dublin Melbourne Johannesburg and Madras*

SBN 333 14928 9

Printed in Great Britain by
WESTERN PRINTING SERVICES LTD
Bristol

Contents

Preface		vii
One	Introduction	1
Two	Fixed *v*. Flexible Interest Rates	8
Three	How Roll-Over Credits are Arranged	21
Four	Terms of the Contracts	29
Five	How Interest Rates are Adjusted	35
Six	What Determines the Spread?	41
Seven	Terms of Repayment	52
Eight	Currency Options	58
Nine	The Secondary Market	63
Ten	The Boom in Roll-Over Credits	68
Eleven	Effect on Growth	75
Twelve	Is it Inflation?	81
Thirteen	Impact on Foreign Exchanges	87
Fourteen	The Official Attitude	93
Fifteen	Prospects for Roll-Over Credits	99
Index		105

Preface

It seems to be my destiny to write books on hitherto neglected subjects. Before the Second World War I wrote the first book on forward exchange; after the war I wrote the first book on primitive money. In the sixties I produced the first book on Euro-dollars; in the middle sixties the first history of foreign exchange. All these subjects have now a sizeable literature, and so has the Euro-bond market – a subject on which I wrote a book in the middle sixties. There is something satisfying in doing pioneer work, navigating uncharted seas. So I am always on the lookout for some new subject.

I found that in spite of the spectacular expansion of roll-over credits – medium-term credits with adjustable interest rates – very little has been written about the system. Articles appeared occasionaly in the quarterly reviews published by banks and in magazines on currency and banking – I myself had an unsigned article in the November–December 1972 issue of *International Currency Review* – and a survey of the past month's events appears regularly in *Euro-Money*. But no attempt has been made until now to examine the practice in detail and to investigate its broader implications.

It is the object of this book to fill this gap in financial

literature. Its material has been collected through personal interviews with a large number of bankers and brokers actively engaged in roll-over credit operations. My thanks are due to all of them for their contribution to the material which I have collected. The task of bringing the facts together was relatively easy. What proved more difficult was to try to reconcile conflicting factual information and to choose between conflicting interpretations.

I had to deal with such problems when preparing my previous books also. After all, no banker and no broker is in a position to keep an eye on the whole market, and their experiences are apt to differ one from the other. But in the field of roll-over credits the discrepancies are infinitely more pronounced. Although it may be an exaggeration to say that there has never been two identically termed roll-over credit contracts, their terms do differ widely; and so do the practices applied by various quarters. So in order to avoid criticism by those who, being actively engaged in roll-over credits, may find some statements in this book about terms, techniques or practices which they may not have encountered, may I hasten to reassure them that the passage that is unfamiliar to them would not have been included in this book if I had not been informed of its substance by someone who had actually encountered it in his practical experience.

What I am afraid of is that from time to time I generalised information on practices which were in fact only applied in isolated instances. My interpretations, too, might have been faulty. Nevertheless I deemed it worthwhile to risk such mistakes in order to draw atten-

tion to the various aspects of the subject which have not yet been examined adequately. Perhaps my mistakes will make it easier for others to discover the correct answers.

This brings me to a personal aspect of my pioneer work. A well-known professor of economics recently told a mutual friend that I am his *bête noire*, because I have written all the books *he* had wanted to write. But what had prevented him from writing them? And what prevents him from writing another book on a subject on which I have written one? There is room for more than one book on any subject, and I do not flatter myself by assuming that my book has completely exhausted its subject. He could and should write a bigger and better book. Anyhow, all situations keep changing and need to be examined from different viewpoints. So I do not feel guilty of blocking the progress of the younger generation by being still actively engaged in my 76th year in searches for original subjects. It is certainly a case of free-for-all, and let the best man win!

London   P.E.
March 1973

PUBLISHER'S NOTE: Paul Einzig died on May 8, 1973, aged 75, while this, his last book, was in the press.

CHAPTER ONE

Introduction

The subject of this book is the system of medium-term credits with adjustable interest rates. Instead of fixing the interest rate for the entire period of a credit, it is adjusted from time to time, at fixed intervals, to the ever-changing market rates on inter-bank deposits. This new system may also be described as credits with flexible interest rates, or as credits with variable interest rates. Because a high proportion of them are handled by a consortium of banks and are placed with a syndicate of banks, they are often referred to as consortium credits or syndicated credits. But neither heading would cover the entire subject, because in a great many instances single banks grant such credits to their clients.

The popular name for such credits, whether granted by single banks or by large international groups of banks, whether they assume the form of book credits or of international note issues, is 'roll-over credits', presumably because, even though they are granted for a period of years, they are automatically renewed on modified terms every six months or such other short period as is fixed in the contract. The credit is thus 'rolled-over' from one interest period to another until it matures.

Roll-over credits constitute an innovation attributed to the London banking community, the initiators of Euro-dollars and other innovations. There has been a remarkable number of such innovations in recent years.

The third quarter of the twentieth century witnessed an amazing evolution in the sphere of international finance. While structural changes during the last quarter of the nineteenth century and the first half of the twentieth century were gradual and few and far between, the structural evolution of the system during the early post-war period was rather slow, it became greatly accelerated during the late fifties and the years that followed.

Up to the middle fifties the international monetary system was substantially the same as it had emerged from the war and had been adjusted by the application of the Bretton Woods system. Not until the late fifties did the emergence and expansion of the Euro-dollar system introduce the first institutional change of fundamental importance. It was soon followed by other institutional innovations – the emergence of parallel money market, the market in dollar Certificates of Deposits, the various Euro-currency markets, the inter-bank sterling deposit market, the market in sterling Certificates of Deposits, the Euro-bond market and other Euro-issue markets, the use of multiple currencies and composite currencies, the creation of multi-national banks and the spectacular increase in the number of foreign bank branches and affiliates in all banking centres and in fiscal havens.

The duopoly of London and New York as world banking centres became less distinct. Strong financial

centres emerged or gained prominence – in Europe: Frankfurt, Paris, the Swiss centres, Amsterdam, Brussels, Luxembourg, Vienna; Montreal and Toronto in Canada; Nassau, Beirut, Singapore, Hong Kong, Tokyo, Johannesburg, etc., on the other continents. Co-operation between banks at the various centres in the issue of international loans and the arrangement of international credits became much closer. The large number of new banks worked at times in close harmony with many old-established institutions. At times there was fierce competition between the multitude of banks, old and new. All of them were determined to earn their increased overheads and to make a reasonable profit in addition.

One of the most important changes has been the evolution and expansion of the system of roll-over credits – medium-term credits with variable interest rates which are adjusted at fixed intervals to changes in the current market rates for short-term credits. This device constitutes an innovation from three distinct points of view. It has greatly expanded the use of medium-term bank credits. It has introduced the system of flexible interest rates. And it has adopted the system of syndication of bank credits between a number of banks. Neither of these changes constitutes an absolute innovation, but the difference in the degree of their application is so extensive that it amounts to a difference in kind.

Medium-term bank credits, as distinct from medium-term public issues or private placings of bonds, were until recently very little known. Various official reports criticised the banking system on the ground of the inadequacy of the extent to which it provided the economy with medium-term credits. While short-term

credits were provided in the form of loans, overdrafts, acceptance credits, etc., and there was a capital market for long-term capital issues, medium-term credits were until comparatively recently difficult to obtain. After the war the situation improved, and medium-term credits became more easily obtainable, especially in the form of Euro-currency deposits for periods of up to seven years or Euro-bonds for similar periods.

The development of medium-term inter-bank deposit markets in dollars, sterling or other leading currencies went a long way towards enabling banks to meet their clients' requirements for medium-term credits, because they were in a position to undo their commitments by means of borrowing offsetting deposits of more or less corresponding maturities. But most of the markets in medium-term deposits were narrow and each transaction was a matter of negotiation. These markets did not expand sufficiently to meet the rapidly increasing requirements for medium-term credits. Such requirements increased because of the expansion of the production and sale of capital goods. The production and sale of capital equipments, means of transport such as planes or ships, tankers and container ships, were financed to a large extent with the aid of medium-term credits.

The difficulty from the point of view of both lenders and borrowers was that towards the late sixties and the early seventies interest rates underwent very wide fluctuations, mostly at a very high level. The extent of their ups and downs was without precedent in modern financial history. This means that lenders and borrowers had to assume considerable risk when committing themselves to a fixed interest rate for a period of years. Simulta-

4

neously with the increase of this risk arising from the possibility of wide changes of interest rates, the periods for which bank credits were granted also became longer. The volume of medium-term credits increased, and the period which came under that definition became longer.

Between them the wider fluctuations of interest rates and the longer maturities of credits gave rise to the system of roll-over credits. It is a highly involved system and its application varies so widely that nobody could possibly claim to be familiar with all practices and techniques. For instance in the course of my enquiries in the City I found that the majority of the specialists I had consulted were unaware that Local Authorities accepted medium-term deposits on roll-over terms adjusted to sterling CD rates.

The present book aims at describing a wide variety of practices, even though I cannot claim to have succeeded in covering the entire field. It also attempts to deal with some of the broader implications of the system. Chapter 2 deals with the relative advantages and disadvantages of flexible and fixed interest rates, a subject which certainly deserves to get as much attention as the much-publicised controversy between advocates of fixed and floating exchange rates.

In Chapter 3 the methods by which roll-over credits are arranged are outlined. It indicates the main forms of the contracts, but the details of the terms of contracts are discussed in Chapter 4. Owing to the wide variety of contracts, this chapter, as most other chapters, is barely more than a sample-survey.

The most important provision of the contracts, the method of the adjustment of interest rates, is discussed in

detail in Chapter 5. It describes the technique of determining the interest rates on each interest date for the next interest period. The adjustment is usually based on the London Euro-dollar rate, while the spread – the differential between that rate and the rate actually payable by the borrower – is fixed in the contract and remains unchanged. The factors influencing the spread are dealt with in Chapter 6. This is probably the most important chapter in the book, both from a practical and from a theoretical point of view.

The terms of repayment are discussed in Chapter 7, which deals with the early repayment options included in many contracts, enabling borrowers to repay before maturity. Another important option, which enables the borrower to choose between several currencies in which to receive and repay the credit, is examined in Chapter 8.

The next chapter deals with the secondary market in roll-over credits. This is a highly controversial subject because market opinion varies very widely on the question of whether such a market does in fact exist and, if so, how significant it is.

In Chapter 10 is discussed the causes of the sudden expansion of the market in roll-over credits during the late sixties and the early seventies. The next two chapters deal with its effect on economic growth and on inflation. In Chapter 13 we examine the impact of roll-over credits on foreign exchanges, and in Chapter 14 the official attitude towards the new device is discussed. While the authorities welcomed it because of its significance from the point of view of London's position as an international banking centre, they viewed the boom

in roll-over credits with growing concern. But up to the time of writing nothing has been done to check or slow down the boom.

In the concluding chapter an attempt is made to forecast the future development of the system both in normal and in abnormal conditions. Tentative suggestions are made for its possible improvement. The importance of roll-over credits is liable to have its ups and downs. The institution itself has not yet settled down to its definitive form and is subject to variations. Many of its practical and theoretical aspects are highly controversial. It gives rise to many interesting problems which are well worth studying.

CHAPTER TWO

Fixed *v*. Flexible Interest Rates

Amongst the variety of innovations in the sphere of finance since 1945 the increased flexibility of interest rates was the most remarkable change. This assertion will no doubt be contested by those in favour of floating exchanges, who consider the recurrent partial adoption of the policy they advocate as the boldest and most revolutionary change experienced in the monetary sphere in our times. Indeed they fancy themselves as revolutionary reformers and are blissfully unaware that the clown's bells on their revolutionaries' Phrygian caps are audible to everybody but themselves. They are evidently oblivious of the fact that the system of floating exchanges, so far from being a revolutionary reform, is as old as the foreign exchange system itself. By contrast the system of flexible interest rates is a recent revolutionary innovation which dates from the sixties.

Although the controversy that is raging between advocates and opponents of floating exchanges is outside the scope of this book – readers interested in that subject are referred to my book *The Case Against Floating Exchanges* – it is necessary to deal with the subject briefly in order to draw attention to the contrast between

the antiquity of flexible exchanges and the novelty of flexible interest rates.

Apart from a few relatively brief periods, and from a relatively small number of fixed currencies, exchange rates have hardly ever been absolutely fixed. Unless the system of officially pegged rates is adopted, under which the authorities buy and sell exchanges at rigidly fixed rates with a narrow spread between their official buying and selling rates, exchanges have always been subject to the influence of the ever-changing supply–demand relationship and to the effects of any anticipations of changes in that relationship. Admittedly their fluctuation was limited under the gold standard by the automatic operation of the gold export points and gold import points, and under the Bretton Woods system by the maximum and minimum intervention points fixed by Central Banks in agreement with the International Monetary Fund. It is still supposed to be limited under the Smithsonian Agreement, at any rate as far as those countries are concerned which have not departed from that Agreement. Flexible rates are in operation in Britain and other important countries who either do not aim at maintaining stable exchanges as a matter of monetary policy, or who are unable to maintain stable exchanges. In the more remote past, when coins were exchanged against each other, exchange rates were subject to wide fluctuations, because of frequent official or unofficial debasements of the coinages. Gold coins and silver coins fluctuated in terms of each other because of the instability of the gold–silver ratio. In any case the transport of coins was so risky and costly, and the costs were subject to such wide variations that exchange

9

rates fluctuated well beyond their theoretical specie points before the resulting specie movements were able to produce their readjusting effect on exchange rates.

When transactions in coins were supplemented and gradually replaced by transactions in foreign bills of exchange the range of fluctuations remained wide, because the exchange rates depended on the quality of the coins in which the bills were payable. Until comparatively recently the relative metal contents of the coinages of most countries were subject to wide fluctuations, so that there was ample scope for exchange rates between them to float. Nor did matters improve after the adoption of paper currency. Even during periods when they were convertible the value of bills payable in paper currency depended on the ever-changing metallic value of the coins into which they were convertible, and on changes in the prospects of the maintenance of their convertibility. When their convertibility was suspended the value of bills depended largely on the assessment of the prospects of a restoration of their convertibility. Since inconvertible paper money was liable to be inflated the changes in the relative degree of inflation in various countries provided ample scope for wide fluctuations of exchanges.

It was not until the concluding decades of the nineteenth century that the adoption of the gold standard by an increasing number of countries came to introduce a relatively high degree of stability of exchange rates between a number of currencies. Even then the number of currencies which only fluctuated within a very narrow range as a result of the automatic operation of the

gold standard was relatively small. The First World War and its aftermath resulted in an unprecedented degree of instability of exchanges. Those who remember the wide fluctuations of the inter-war period cannot possibly share the conviction of the advocates of floating exchanges that the adoption of the system of their choice constitutes an innovation. Quite on the contrary, it is a relapse into an archaic state of affairs which had existed more or less throughout the ages and which the Bretton Woods Agreement had sought to terminate.

The historic trend had been quite different concerning interest rates. In the distant past interest rates were sought to be kept rigid by the application of severe anti-usury laws which fixed the maximum permissible rates. In more recent times interference with the automatic operation of money market forces by an increasing degree of government intervention aimed, among other things, at reducing the range of fluctuations of interest rates and at keeping them at a level that is considered by the authorities to be in accordance with the requirements of the national economy. This aim was attained to a considerable degree in advanced countries where monetary policy was pursued efficiently. In such countries there was a relatively high degree of rigidity of interest rates, and their adjustment came to be considered in many situations as a necessary evil. Nevertheless there were from time to time substantial changes in interest rates, usually as a result of monetary policy decisions, but often because the authorities were unable to prevent them.

The banks, too, played an important part in the maintenance of relatively stable interest rates. They usually

readily followed voluntarily the advice received from official quarters, and were willing to curtail fluctuations of interest rates by the adoption of cartels restraining free competition amongst themselves in their capacity of lenders or borrowers. It had been a well-established practice to lend at fixed interest rates for definite periods, even though rates allowed on deposits subject to notice were adjusted to Bank-rate changes.

There is a great deal to be said in favour of maintaining stable interest rates, but the case for stability in this sphere is not nearly as unanswerable as in respect of the stability of exchanges. Fluctuations of interest rates are not as disturbing to the economy, or even to business firms, as are fluctuations of exchange rates. Admittedly, the former are also apt to cause considerable inconvenience and, apart from inflicting losses on borrowers, tend to discourage business activity. But wide exchange movements are liable to entail much graver consequences, apart from other reasons, because instead of being self-correcting, they are very often self-aggravating.

Changes in interest rates produce their normal effects – they encourage or discourage borrowing or lending. Undue rigidity of interest rates is apt to create highly artificial situations. Adjustment of interest rates is the natural way of mitigating speculative booms and of reviving business activity during depressions. A similar result may also be admitted by an adjustment of exchange rates. But the disturbing effects of that device is much more pronounced, its result is much more doubtful, and it operates much more slowly.

It was probably the realisation of the advantages of some degree of elasticity of interest rates that induced

the United States authoritites to mitigate Regulation Q which fixes the maximum interest rates that American banks are permitted to pay on deposits. Although at the time of writing small deposits and deposits maturing within thirty days are still subject to such limitation, rates on other deposits can now be changed freely.

A somewhat similar change occurred in the United Kingdom as a result of the abolition of the clearing banks' cartel which had fixed 'base rates'. The replacement of the traditional Bank rate by the more flexible 'official minimum lending rate' was a step in the same direction.

All these changes occurred in the late sixties or early seventies. By far the most important change towards more flexible interest rates in advanced countries was, however, the increasing adoption of the system of roll-over credits, which came to introduce a high degree of flexibility of the cost of medium-term credits.

Apart from the institutional changes outlined above, the basic economic trend itself made for wider fluctuations of interest rates. Inflation has been on the increase in every country, even though it has been progressing at a different rate and apart from the rate at which prices are rising, which itself is subject to variations. The extent to which the public has become inflation-conscious is apt to influence the interest rate at which lenders are prepared to lend and borrowers are prepared to borrow. The growing uncertainty that the prospect of inflation engenders and its effect on interest rates is one of the causes of wider fluctuations of interest rates in terms of the current monetary unit, and even in real terms.

Those who expect an escalation of inflation are prepared to pay higher rates and prefer to borrow for longer periods. But rises in interest are not necessarily an uninterrupted process. From time to time there are periods of decline. The uncertainty of interest rate prospects tends to make both lenders and borrowers reluctant at times to commit themselves to a fixed interest rate for a relatively long period. Amidst such circumstances the advent of the system of roll-over credits – a system under which interest rates are adapted in certain intervals to the current rates prevailing in the market – met with favourable response and became increasingly popular.

There is, of course, room for two opinions on the question of whether the relaxation of the rigidity of interest rates constitutes progress in the right direction or whether it is yet another manifestation of the deplorable relaxation of discipline in the economic sphere. Dogmatic believers in the all-curing effect of *laissez-faire* are unhesitatingly in favour of freely fluctuating interest rates in the same way as they are in favour of freely fluctuating exchanges. The merits or demerits of the roll-over credit must not be judged, however, on the basis of dogmatic approval or disapproval of an unhampered operation of free market forces.

Nor should the system be condemned – as it often is in orthodox banking circles – because it is greatly misused. After all, any system is liable to be misused. Overtrading and irresponsible lending in the form of roll-over credits is admittedly prevalent. More will be said about it in a later chapter. But such misuse is not inherent in the system, any more than it was inherent in

the system of acceptance credits in the late twenties.

The main argument in favour of the device of adjustable interest rates is that it enables borrowers to abstain from committing themselves for long periods to interest rates which they consider to be too high. As far as lenders are concerned, they are in a position to hedge against losses that might result from an increase in interest rates by re-borrowing the amounts lent for the periods in question. In this way they are able to act according to their expectations of changes in interest rates. If they expect a fall or no change in interest rates they prefer to abstain from hedging. If they hedge and subsequently change their opinion about the prospects of interest rates, they are in a position to undo the hedge by re-lending the amount borrowed. Apart altogether from their views about the prospects, they might prefer to assume no commitments and be content with the profit represented by the differential between lending and borrowing rates.

It is the borrowers who are exposed under the system of fixed interest rates to losses caused by a decline in interest rates. They have, of course, no means for hedging by re-lending the money borrowed because they need the money. Admittedly they would stand to benefit by a rise in interest rates that might occur during the period of their fixed interest bearing medium-term loans, for their rivals who had preferred roll-over credits might now have to pay higher interest rates, while they themselves would have the benefit of the lower fixed interest rates. But borrowing at relatively high fixed interest rates for periods of years is also a gamble which exposes the borrowers to the risk of being

undersold by their rivals, who are able to borrow later at a much lower interest rate. This was a matter of small importance when fluctuations of interest rates amounted to a bare fraction of one per cent. But nowadays the range of fluctuations over a period of five years might well be 5 per cent, or even more.

In the case of short-term financing of the production or purchase of goods with a quick turnover, the risk of changes in interest rates does not arise in an essential way. But if the financing of a transaction calls for medium-term credits, the system of roll-over credits gives the borrower the chance of a choice, which enables him to act in accordance with his expectations concerning prospects of interest rates. If he expects a fall in interest rates, he resorts to roll-over credit arrangements. If he expects a rise, he borrows at a fixed rate. His expectations might well prove to have been wrong, but, at any rate, he has a chance to act according to them.

Admittedly the availability of roll-over credit facilities need not safeguard business firms from being placed at a disadvantage to their rivals. If interest rates rise, they have to pay higher rates for each consecutive interest period, while their rivals having borrowed at low fixed rates will be at an advantage. Of course, if borrowers expect a decline in interest rates, even in the absence of the roll-over credit system, they have the alternative of borrowing for short-term in the hope that they would be able to renew the credit again and again at more favourable interest rates. But that method would involve the risk of being unable to renew their credits at all in the event of an unforeseen credit

squeeze apart altogether from the risk of having to pay higher renewal rates.

A large and increasing proportion of production and distribution of goods requires medium-term financing. In addition to capital goods which call for long-term capital issues, a great many firms produce or buy capital goods which can be financed with the aid of medium-term credits. Such goods include aircraft, giant tankers, container ships, etc. And even firms which are fully provided with capital to finance their equipment may be in need of medium-term credits, for the sake of being able to adopt long-term production programmes. The advantages of planning well ahead are being increasingly realised. In order to be able to plan ahead it is necessary to ensure in advance the availability of the financial resources required for the entire period. The entire amount is not needed immediately, and under many roll-over credit contracts it is paid to the borrower in instalments fixed in advance, or it is left to the borrower to draw on the credit as and when required. Even if the cost of the future instalments of credit is uncertain, its availability is assured.

The roll-over credit system is one of the recently adopted sophisticated systems which have greatly increased the importance of the treasurer or the finance director. In the old, simple days production programmes were elaborated by the board with the aid of the production manager and the sales manager; the treasurer was only consulted at a later stage. His role was confined to raising the necessary funds after the decisions were taken. Today the treasurer is called in for consultation at a very early stage so that he may advise

the board or executive about the possibility of raising the necessary funds in a way that keeps down the cost of financing to a minimum.

An argument against using roll-over credits is that they increase the difficulties of costing. Interest charges are uncertain, and a sharp rise in interest rates is liable to add considerably to the costs. For this reason roll-over credits are used preferably for the financing of goods with a high profit margin, so as to avoid the risk of converting a narrow profit margin into a loss because of the increase of interest rates.

Neither fixed nor flexible interest charges can eliminate or even mitigate the risk derived from changes in real interest rates as distinct from nominal interest rates – that is, interest charges in terms of purchasing power and in terms of constant monetary unit. Lenders are exposed to losses through a depreciation of the monetary unit in which interest and principal are payable. In theory borrowers stand to benefit by a depreciation of the monetary unit, but in practice a rise in prices is not necessarily accompanied by a rise in the income or in the value of assets of every debtor. There can be no certainty that the prices of goods financed by borrowed money will rise in accordance with the increase of the general price level.

Very broadly speaking, interest rates tend to rise with the increase of prices and they tend to fall with the decline of prices. Thinking in terms of averages, this would lead to the conclusion that borrowers of roll-over credits can afford to pay the higher interest rates caused by the rise in the prices of their goods, and that lenders derive compensation for the decline of interest rates through

the increase of the purchasing power of their money. In practice interest rates are liable to rise or fall for many reasons unconnected with the depreciation and appreciation of the monetary unit of the credit, and in any case, as already observed, individual lenders or borrowers may be affected differently by the changes in the average price levels.

Although banks are able to hedge against the interest rate risk by re-lending the money borrowed or re-borrowing the money lent, the new system offers them an alternative device. Since they have many commitments both ways as lenders or borrowers, they are only concerned with the net balance between their grand total of borrowing and their grand total of lending. Being familiar with various parallel markets in various centres, to which their customers have no direct access, they are able to hedge and undo hedges at a relatively low cost.

Borrowers of roll-over credits with an option to repay them at some relatively early date are in a position to replace their credits by credits with fixed interest, if and when they should come to expect a rise in interest rates. Roll-over credits have made medium-term credit facilities more adaptable to changing requirements. They stimulate borrowing and lending when borrowers and/ or lenders are reluctant to commit themselves to the prevailing interest rates. These facilities may be used as an alternative to credit facilities with fixed interest rates, but they may be additional to them, in which case the total volume of borrowing – especially of medium-term borrowing – increases.

From the point of view of banks, it is not necessarily convenient for them to exhaust a high proportion of

their borrowing capacity to hedge against roll-over credits for the sake of a relatively narrow profit margin. But if they take the view that interest rates will increase it may be worth their while to lend roll-over credits without hedging, so as to be able to benefit by the subsequent rise in interest rates.

From a broader point of view the application of roll-over credits ensures a speedier adjustment of interest rates to changes in current money supply–demand relationships. With the increase in the proportion of medium-term credits fixed interest means that an unduly small proportion of interest charges would respond speedily to changes in interest rates. Thanks to roll-over credits, a much larger proportion responds to them. This means an increase in the influence of changes in interest rates as a means for restoring or adjusting equilibrium.

CHAPTER THREE

How Roll-Over Credits are Arranged

Roll-over credits may assume various forms and are therefore arranged in various ways. A large number of relatively small individual transactions – the total of which probably represents a high percentage of the grand total of roll-over credits – are concluded simply between banks and their customers in the ordinary way in which bank credits are arranged. The main difference being that the borrower has to agree with the bank manager on the formula with which interest rates are periodically adjusted.

No statistical information is of course available about the approximate total of such credits, since they are concluded entirely without any publicity, and neither the monthly returns of banks to the Bank of England nor even their own annual balance sheets discriminate between such credits and conventional credits with fixed interest rates. But it is widely understood in banking circles that the fashion of adjustable interest rates has caught on to such an extent that the grand total of un-publicised roll-over bank credits is estimated at a very high figure. Indeed the view is held in some banking circles that the published amounts of roll-over credits, substantial as they are – they reached $12 billion in 1972 – are barely more than the tip of the iceberg, even

though in other quarters this is considered to be a mild exaggeration.

The unpublicised credits usually assume the form of letters of credit in which the maximum amount, the maximum period, and the terms on which the interest rate is subject to adjustment, are set out. The borrower has often the option to draw upon the credit in instalments as and when he requires the money. The interest rates are determined on the basis of the interest rates prevailing at the time of the conclusion of the credit or of the first drawing, and on subsequent 'interest dates' increased by an additional percentage called 'spread' which under most contracts remains unchanged even though the basic interest rate may move up or down with market rates.

If such transactions are fixed by a routine arrangement, it need not call for a long and involved contract, for the two parties know each other and trust each other, so that they do not deem it necessary to insert cumbersome clauses to 'stop all possible loopholes'. Nevertheless many contracts between banker and customer contain many more safeguarding provisions than is customary in ordinary bank credits, especially if the amount is substantial. The lending banks may envisage the possibility of subsequently granting participation to other banks in the transaction. For the sake of meeting the probable requirements for safeguards of banks which are not familiar with the borrower, they might deem it expedient to insert in the contracts additional terms to satisfy a consortium that might take over the bulk of the credit. If such a consortium participates from the very outset then the terms have to be agreed upon in advance to

the satisfaction of all participants. Such contracts are necessarily longer and more complicated, since they would have to be passed by the lawyers and accountants of several banks. All that would take time, so the negotiations would take longer.

An alternative way of arranging roll-over credits is for the borrowing firm or institution or authority to issue notes and sell them to a managing bank or a consortium of managing banks, which in turn sells them to a syndicate of banks and other financial institutions. Each one of them takes over a relatively small amount which it would be able to keep in its own portfolio or would be able to place with its own customers, so that no public issue would be necessary.

Another alternative procedure is the conclusion of an agreement by the managing banks with the borrower; in this case photocopies of the contract are circulated among potential members of the syndicate: or a Placing Memorandum containing the essential terms may be circulated. In many instances the managing banks issue Participation Certificates which are underwritten, in the same way as Euro-bonds, by a syndicate consisting of some dozens of banks and other dealers or institutional investors. Their number is anything up to fifty, or even higher. While in many instances the terms are negotiated by the managing banks and the potential members of the syndicate are offered participation on terms that are already fixed, in other instances members of the syndicate – or at any rate those who are prepared to take large amounts – have some say in the negotiation of the terms. Sometimes the managing banks, knowing as they do the particular requirements of leading potential

members of the syndicate, insist on the insertion of terms without which the banks concerned would not be likely to participate. Often all members of the syndicate are given a chance to state any objections or conditions they may have, and once an agreement is reached the contract is signed by all of them. Bearing as they do some fifty signatures, such contracts look like King Charles's Death Warrant. The publicised announcement of the transactions, complete with the names of all participants, is often referred to in the City, for some obscure reason, as 'thumbstones'.

Occasionally roll-over credits assume the form of promissory notes, which are one-name papers bought from the borrowers and placed by the managing banks with the syndicates of lenders. Promissory notes are usually short-term papers and they are discounted at a rate fixed for the whole period. Roll-over promissory notes which mature in terms of years are discounted on their interest dates once in six months for the next period of six months at the current commercial paper rates. As in the case with all notes arising from roll-over credits, holders have no recourse to the original buyer who had re-sold them to the new buyers or to any subsequent seller. The fact that the seller of notes disclaims all responsibility for the payment of interest and repayment of principal is made quite clear in the text of all notes.

Many roll-over credit transactions are arranged with banks through the intermediary of money brokers, a small number of whom specialise in this type of business. This method is followed mostly when money is tight and borrowers prefer to leave to the brokers the task of finding a lender instead of exposing themselves to direct

refusals until they can find a bank prepared to undertake the transaction. When money is plentiful borrowers have no difficulty in finding banks that are able and willing to take charge of the transaction. Indeed in a borrowers' market potential borrowers of good standing literally have thrust upon them credits which banks are eager to grant them.

If roll-over credits are publicised at all the announcements contain the bare outline of the transactions – the amount involved, the maximum period, the names of the managing banks, the consortium and the members of the syndicate. They seldom contain additional details, because they are publicised for the record only, not as an invitation for subscription. The entire amount has been placed privately with the syndicate by the time the notice is published.

Banks usually participate in each others' note issues on a basis of reciprocity. They take a few millions of dollars of each others' issues, even on occasions when they are not enthusiastic about the terms or about the borrowers' standing, on the assumption that the managing banks, on their part, will take from them a similar amount of comparable issues.

Many members of the syndicate are not big enough to assume the role of managing banks. They may not even specialise in such transactions. In their case the reason why they choose to participate in not particularly attractive transactions is that it adds to their prestige to be associated with a number of first-class banks.

The negotiation of syndicated credits is apt to take many months as it is often difficult to reach a compromise which is acceptable to a sufficient number of

lenders to cover the amount required as well as to the borrower. Because of the large number of people necessarily involved in the negotiations it would be difficult to prevent the leakage of information. This is one of the reasons for the practice of announcing the transaction as soon as agreement is reached on its terms. No details are published in the announcement, however. The reason that some borrowers want publicity is because of the fact that so many prominent banks participate in the transaction and this is apt to benefit the borrower's prestige.

Even if no part of the issue is placed in the United States, in many instances the managing banks feel the need to comply with American legal requirements, just in case some of the holders should want to place their notes there later. On the other hand, some notes make it quite clear that they are not registered under the Securities Act of 1932 of the United States.

Many banks may insist on the inclusion of particular terms for which they have preferences. If their requirements conflict with each other they have to be reconciled, and the resulting compromise has to be accepted by the borrower. The length and nature of the contracts, which are discussed in the next chapter, depend to a high degree on the nationality of the managing banks and on the countries where the notes are meant to be placed. Continental contracts are shorter than British contracts, and the latter are shorter than American contracts. When American banks participate to a considerable extent the contracts are usually very long and detailed, because they include detailed information required by the Securities Exchange Commission. A number of clauses aim at stopping every possible legal

loophole. Lawyers and accountants take an active part in the drafting of the contracts once the bankers have agreed on their major provisions. When the contract is signed an 'executive date' – the day on which the agents deliver the contracts signed by all parties – is fixed.

The usual commission which the borrowers pay to the managing banks is apt to change. It is at the time of writing (1973) $1\frac{1}{2}$ per cent, while the latter pay $\frac{1}{2}$ per cent to the dealers. All participants transfer their contribution to the credit – or to the instalment of the credit which the borower is to receive – to the agents, as and when the borrower draws on it. If this is not fixed in the contract the borrower has to give the agents the agreed notice, usually five days.

Standard amounts of the notes are usually but not necessarily $1000, $10,000 $100,000 and $500,000. Holders of notes are usually entitled to ask the agents or the managing banks to split the nominal amounts of the notes into smaller denominations of round amounts, and this is done without any charge.

The originally negotiated terms are stated in the Preliminary Placing Memorandum, but they are subject to amendments as a result of requests by potential participants of importance. In some instances the members of the syndicate are required to give an informal assurance that they do not at present contemplate disposing of the notes. Bearer notes may change hands without any restriction, but many registered notes can only be transferred with the managing banks' approval. The latter often prefer to take over the notes, and this is done on the basis of the prevailing interest rates. In such

instances the 'secondary market' consists mainly of the managing banks.

The role of agents is regulated in great detail. They relieve the managing banks and the borrowers of the burden of dealing with the contributions of participants, with the payment of interest and the repayment of the principal. If the number of participants is large the amount of clerical work involved is considerable.

CHAPTER FOUR

Terms of the Contracts

While it would be an exaggeration to suggest that the conditions of every contract are different from those of all other contracts, there is certainly an immense variety of conditions. Each managing bank has a favourite formula which differs in many respects from that of other managing banks. What is more, these formulas are subject to modifications to meet the wishes of borrowers and those of other participating banks. When roll-over credits are a borrowers' market the managing banks are willing to meet the wishes of borowers to a very considerable extent, for otherwise their less rigid competitors might outbid them. On such occasions the managing banks are inclined to resist the demands of other banks for changes of the terms, because, unless the contract is particularly unacceptable, a sufficient number of banks are willing to go out of their way to participate. Conversely when roll-over credits are a lenders' market, borrowers are not in a strong enough position to dictate the terms, while the managing banks have to go out of their way to meet potential participants' objections.

Having regard to the absence of any standardised forms of contracts such as exist in other markets, and

to the wide variety of points on which the various parties are apt to feel strongly, it is indeed remarkable how an agreement can ever be reached at all on all the terms between lenders and borrowers, and between the various lenders. Eventually some progress might be made towards the adoption of a certain number of standardised contracts, but the achievement of anything like uniformity is simply inconceivable.

The following are the most important terms of the contracts:

(1) The amount of the credit.
(2) The maturity date (or dates), or other terms of of the drawdown.
(3) The terms of repayment.
(4) The basic interest rate.
(5) The 'spread' between the basic interest rate and the actual interest charge payable by the debtor.
(6) The various commissions and expenses.
(7) The currency of denomination.
(8) Interest periods.
(9) Options of early repayment.
(10) Currency options.
(11) Guarantees.
(12) Methods of adjustment of the interest rate.
(13) Role of managing banks.
(14) Role of agents.
(15) Role of reference banks.
(16) Method of interest payments.
(17) Provisions concerning taxes.
(18) Changes in the situation that would relieve lenders of their obligations under the contract.
(19) Default on interest payments.

(20) Determination of the legislation which applies to the contract.

(21) Provisions in the event of disputes.

(22) Information to be provided by the borrower.

(23) Denomination of the notes.

The amount of individual transactions of roll-over bank credits is in many instances small compared with that of consortium credits which is usually substantial. It may be payable in one sum, or in several instalments fixed in the contract, or its 'drawdown' may be left to the borrower's discretion, subject to notice prescribed in the contract. The borrower is usually under no obligation to use the whole amount of the credit granted.

The contract always fixes the maximum period for which the credit is granted. It also fixes the schedule of maturities if it is repayable in instalments. In some contracts the borrower, having repaid part of the credit, is entitled to draw on it again, within the limits of the maximum maturity.

The basic rate is the current Euro-dollar rate (or other currency rate) quoted for six months' deposits in the London market, or in some other market (or for other deposits, according to the interest period) at the time of the transaction. The basic rate is subject to change between one interest date and the next.

A most important provision fixes the 'spread' between the basic rate and the actual rate of interest payable by the borrower. As will be seen in Chapter 6 that spread varies according to the borrower's credit rating, and is subject to a variety of influences. While the basic rate is adjusted to changes in market rates,

the spread remains unchanged during the whole duration of the credit, unless its adjustment is stipulated in the contract.

The commission paid by the borrower to the managing banks, and by the managing banks to the members of the syndicate and to the agents, is fixed in the contract. So is the 'commitment fee' payable by the debtor on the unused amount of the credit.

Most contracts determine the currency in which the credit is to be granted and repaid and in which interest is payable. But in a number of contracts the borrower has the choice between several currencies, or the credit is fixed in terms of a composite currency unit. If the borrower has the option to choose between various currencies, the contract prescribes the exact way in which that option may be exercised, and the circumstances in which the borrower is restricted in the choice of currencies is stipulated in the contract.

The contract fixes the duration of the 'interest periods', the periods for which the interest rate is fixed in advance on the date of the implementation of the contract and on the subsequent 'interest dates'.

Contracts may contain options for early repayment, subject to notice being given by the borrower to the agent and subject to the payment of a 'penalty'. The length of the notice is fixed in the contract. Lenders are not in a position to claim early repayment unless certain abnormal situations arise which are provided for in the contract.

The borrower may be given the choice between several currencies in which to receive the whole or part of the credit. Interest and principal are always repay-

able in the same currency in which the credit is received.

The credit may be secured by a guarantee of a Government or of a Government-controlled institution, or by the parent company of the affiliate which raises the loan, or by some other firm or institution. Multinational concerns and other large firms have affiliates in foreign financial centres for the purpose of raising credits under the parent company's guarantee.

The interest rate is determined on the interest date for the next interest period, on the basis of the current market rate of deposits in terms of the currency of the credit, plus the spread. The exact method by which that interest rate is arrived at is prescribed in the contract.

The rights and obligations of the managing banks are determined in the contracts, and so are the duties of the agents and the 'reference banks' which provide the managing banks with the current quotations of interest rates on interest dates.

Contracts contain provisions concerning taxation in the borrower's country. Usually it is stipulated that the lender is to receive interest payment free of any deduction of such taxes.

Certain changes in the situation, indicated in the contract, relieve the lenders of their obligation to the borrower, and might even empower them to cancel the contract and claim the repayment of the amount lent. Such situations are likely to arise in case of default, or in case of alterations in exchange control, credit control or taxation measures.

The contract always determines the legislation to which the transaction is subject. It is usually the legislation of the managing bank's country, or if there are

several managing banks, of the country of residence of the managing bank which grants the credit. It may also contain provisions concerning arbitration procedure in case of disputes.

The borrower has to provide certain information at the time of the granting of the credits, and also subsequently any other information prescribed in the contract.

Although the denomination of the notes is usually left to the discretion of the managing banks, in some contracts the amounts are stipulated, even though the managing banks reserve the right to split larger units into smaller units.

Appendices to the contracts contain balance sheets and other relevant information concerning the borrowing firm's business. They may contain statistical and other information dealing with the borrower's business or the country in which it is situated together with other material enabling the lender to assess the borrower's position and prospects.

CHAPTER FIVE

How Interest Rates are Adjusted

Once the principle that in given circumstances the systematic adjustment of interest rates on medium-term credits at fixed intervals is justified and advantageous during the duration of the credit, there remains to be examined the question of deciding what method of adjustment should be applied. The system of roll-over credits is not the only means of adjustment. It is possible, for example, to make provision in the contract itself for different interest rates to apply from certain dates. For instance in a number of contracts a certain interest rate is fixed up to, say, three years, and a different interest rate thereafter. Such contracts existed long before the adoption of the roll-over credit system.

Usually the interest rate was fixed higher as from a certain date. This is in accordance with the prevailing practice of charging higher interest rates for longer periods, not necessarily because a rise in interest rates is to be expected, but because the risk is greater if the money is tied down for longer periods. The outlook is more uncertain, and the likelihood of a deterioration of the individual borrower's position or of the general economic situation is higher on credits for seven years than for credits for three years. The rate at which the

interest rate is fixed as from a number of years usually corresponds more or less to the difference between the rate obtainable at the time of lending for the different maturities.

This formula does not solve the problems which roll-over credits are intended to solve, that is, to adjust the interest rate on the credits to the changes in current market rates. For one thing when using this formula the rate is changed at long intervals, usually once or perhaps twice during the duration of the credit. Under the terms of roll-over credits the rate is usually changed every six months, or some other relatively brief period fixed by the contract. What is perhaps even more important is that changes in fixed interest rates are not likely to correspond to changes in market rates. Any anticipation of long-term changes is likely to be proved to have been mistaken. It is possible that interest rates in the market might be lower in three years' time than they are at the time of lending, in which case the pre-arranged increase of the rate at the end of three years produces an even more unrealistic situation than would prevail for loans with fixed, unchanged rates which operate for the entire period.

In theory it is conceivable that in anticipation of a decline in interest rates the fixed rates might be reduced after a number of years, and this rule might be applied when interest rates are abnormally high. Borrowers and lenders prefer to determine the fixed rate for the whole period on the basis of their expectations of the average rate of the entire period subject to prevailing supply–demand relationship. The formula of agreeing in advance to a definite change in the interest rates after a

certain number of years has never been very popular, though there are a number of instances where its application is justified.

Nor is the formula of frequent changes of interest rates that is applied in roll-over credits applied for medium-term Euro-bonds. This is possibly because Euro-bonds are meant to appeal to investors who are not accustomed to such a sophisticated formula, while roll-over credits are granted by banks to banks, and even if they have a secondary market demand for them is confined to very sophisticated types of investors.

Interest rates on roll-over credits are subject to changes at the end of each 'interest period', on the pre-determined 'interest dates' or 'interest determination dates'. By far the most frequently applied interest period is six months, but three months and twelve months are also quite common. In some contracts provision is made for changing the interest period. There may be broken interest periods if borrowers avail themselves of their right to repay the credit before the next interest date.

The interest dates are usually taken as occurring two clear days before the concluding dates of the interest periods. In financial centres where there are official interest rates the determination of the rate for the next interest period is a simple matter. But in centres without such rates, such as London, the method for fixing the new interest rates is apt to be rather elaborate. The contracts usually contain provisions to safeguard the debtors. In the absence of such provisions the debtor depends on the integrity of the managing banks who determine the new rate, usually by asking a broker

or a bank to quote a rate. If the managing banks are banks of standing the debtor may safely depend on them, for managing banks could ill afford to risk their reputation by fixing rates which depart substantially from the current market rate. As in any market, if a customer who had instructed his broker or banker to buy or sell 'at best' finds it repeatedly a very poor 'best', he transfers his accounts.

A large number of contracts contain provisions under which the managing bank or banks must ask 'neutral' banks, referred to as 'reference banks', for the current quotation of interest rates for the maturity corresponding to the next interest period. There may be more than one reference bank – they are also called 'rate setting banks' – in which case the rate will be the average of their quotations. If some of them are unable to quote rates the average of the rates quoted by the remaining banks will be used. To be on the safe side some contracts provide for six reference banks. If the rates are fixed by the managing banks themselves it is the average of their rates that counts. The contract usually stipulates that the relevant rate is to be the one quoted at noon, or at 11 a.m., London time. If the managing banks are in another financial centre, and the credits are not in terms of Euro-dollars, the rates quoted in the centre concerned may be used. The contract decides whether the rates should be the sellers' rate or the middle rate.

In many contracts the parties safeguard themselves against the use of a distorted rate that is likely to be quoted in any one day, on days before or after weekends, holidays, end of month, quarter or year, or through

some fortuitous circumstance or through the coincidence of several distorting influences. To that end the rate is to be based not on the quotation on one single day but on the average of the quotation of several consecutive business days, usually of three days.

The risk that the managing banks or the debtors might influence the rates on the interest determination dates through operating in the market is virtually non-existent, especially for credits in terms of Euro-dollars which have a very wide market. In theory it is conceivable that the rates of credits in terms of some currency with a much narrower spread between inter-bank buying and selling rates might be manipulated if the amount involved is large enough to make it worthwhile. But if the average of several days is used this might be too costly and too risky, particularly if those engaged in such manipulations do not cover their commitments simultaneously. Banks of standing could ill afford the damage to their reputations which would occur if such manoeuvrings should be discovered.

The fact that the six months' Euro-dollar rate was remarkably steady throughout 1972 is sufficient proof that there have been no such manipulations. Indeed for some unaccountable reason the six months' rate was much steadier than either the longer rates or the shorter rates. There is no reason to believe that the roll-over credit transactions – most of which use six months for their interest periods – have a steadying influence on the six months' rate, nor is there any obvious alternative explanation. It has been suggested that in view of the steadiness of the six months' rate the whole complicated procedure of roll-over credit operations was virtually

unnecessary in 1972, for the rates determined on interest dates differed very slightly from a fixed six months' rate on the date of the issue. But that rate need not necessarily remain steady.

Some contracts provide for an increase of the current spreads and the spread charged for later interest periods. This is based on the assumption that interest rates will increase as a result of tighter money and that this might entail a widening of the spread. But during a period of decline of interest rates, caused by increased liquidity, the corollary to that formula would be a reduction of the spread for later interest periods.

In many contracts the changes in interest rates are not left unlimited. A maximum limit or a minimum limit for the interest rates may be fixed. There are contracts which fix both a maximum limit and a minimum limit. Such limits are usually very wide. I know of an instance in which the range was $6\frac{1}{2}$ per cent to 13 per cent.

When as a result of the change in the market rate the interest rate is changed for the next interest period the new rate is not adjusted precisely to the new market rate or the average of market rates. The new rate is usually rounded up to the nearest ⅛ per cent or ¹⁄₁₆ per cent per annum.

The rates used for adjusting the interest rates on roll-over credits are always those quoted for banks of first-rate standing. In some contracts the borrower has the option of changing the next interest period from one standard period to another. Such a change of period is subject to a notice, usually of five days.

CHAPTER SIX

What Determines the Spread?

The most important and most interesting among the terms of roll-over credit contracts is the spread. This is the difference between the current quotation of the Euro-dollar – or, as the case may be, of some other Euro-currency in terms of which the credit is granted – and the actual interest rate payable by the borrower. On the date when the contract becomes operative and on each interest date the spread is added to the current Euro-dollar rate, and the resulting figure represents the interest payable for the next interest period. In the overwhelming majority of instances the interest is paid at the end of the interest period.

The cost of the credit to the borrower is determined by the current Euro-dollar rate for inter-bank time deposits the maturity of which corresponds to the interest period fixed in the contract, plus the spread. The base rate is subject to fluctuations, but the spread is usually fixed for the duration of the contract – unless arrangement is made for its change after a certain number of years. The profit margin of the lender is determined by the spread, plus any profit he may derive from an increase in the base rate in case he re-borrowed the amount lent for a period longer than the next interest

period. In that event a decline of the base rate reduces the lender's profit and might even convert in into a net loss. To avoid this he might forgo his chances of a profit in excess of the spread by hedging for each interest period. This is done in fact on a large scale, hence the wide market for six months' dollar CDs, which are often used for hedging against such a risk, in preference to Euro-dollars, owing to its lower rate.

The borrower is not in a position to hedge against a rise in the base rate. Although the spread remains unchanged he has to pay a higher rate for each interest period for which the current quotation of the Euro-dollar deposit rate is higher than it was when the loan contract became operative. On the other hand he stands to derive profit from a decline of the base rate.

The Euro-dollar rate depends to some extent on the volume of supply and demand in roll-over credits, because a large and increasing proportion of Euro-dollar deposits borrowed by banks is re-lent in the form of roll-over credits. But it must be borne in mind that banks which grant roll-over credits need not necessarily buy dollar deposits in the Euro-dollar market in order to re-lend to the borrowers. They may already possess the dollars required, or they may buy dollars in the foreign exchange market, or they may sell or issue Euro-bonds, or London dollar CDs, or they may use maturing Euro-dollar deposits they had lent. Moreover at least part of the roll-over credits are liable to find their way back, directly or indirectly, into the Euro-dollar pool, though not necessarily immediately the money is borrowed. So it would be a mistake to assume that the pool of Euro-dollar deposits potentially avail-

able in the market, or the amount actually offered at any given moment, becomes reduced to an extent corresponding exactly or even approximately to the amount of the newly-granted roll-over credits in excess of roll-over credit repayments.

The spread is fixed usually for the duration of the credit transaction, though in some contracts it is reduced as from a certain interest date. Over a period the rates quoted to new borrowers are subject to changes, and at times their reduction is sufficiently substantial to make it worth while for debtors to avail themselves of an option clause in their contracts to repay their roll-over credits and re-borrow the amount from the same lender or from some other lender. At any given moment different rates are quoted to different categories of borrowers.

The spread is liable to follow certain basic trends, in addition to being subject to certain short-term influences. The following is a list of the factors that are liable to affect the spread:

(1) The supply of credit available in general or for medium-term credits in particular.
(2) The demand for medium-term credits.
(3) The level of interest rates.
(4) Expectations of changes in interest rates for subsequent interest periods.
(5) Terms on which lenders can hedge.
(6) Keenness of competition among lenders.
(7) Assessment of the credit risk by lenders.
(8) Credit rating of individual borrowers.
(9) Extent of their outstanding indebtedness.
(10) Exchange control risk.

(11) Exchange rate risk or the cost of covering it.

(12) Options and other terms of the contract.

The supply of medium-term credits depends largely on the volume of general liquidity. When money is tight banks are less willing to tie down their resources for relatively long periods, even if they finance the transactions by means of re-borrowing the amount. The availability and cost of facilities for hedging by means of borrowing offsetting deposits, and in given situations by means of forward exchange transactions, affect the supply of roll-over credits. The policies pursued by banks are amongst the main factors affecting the supply of medium-term credits in general and of roll-over credits in particular.

The demand for roll-over credits depends first and foremost on business conditions and prospects in general. But only certain types of business transactions are financed by medium-term credits. The demand depends not only on the volume of medium-term transactions but also on the relative advantage of financing them by means of roll-over credits or, alternatively, by raising long-term capital. The decision depends largely on the view borrowers take on the long-term prospects of interest rates. To some extent an increase in the supply of roll-over credit facilities readily available creates additional demand, owing to the ease with which borrowers are able to satisfy their requirements of that type of credit facilities.

One of the influences that tends to moderate demand for roll-over credits is the complicated and lengthy negotiations that precede the conclusion of each transaction. It takes as much time to negotiate a roll-over

credit as it takes to negotiate a Euro-bond issue. If would-be borrowers have alternative facilities at their disposal which are more easily negotiable, this consideration might divert some demand from the roll-over credit market in spite of the obvious advantages of roll-over credits.

Of course it is incomparably easier for borrowers to negotiate ordinary bank credits, but for medium-term requirements such credits would have to be renewed again and again. There would be the risk that as a result of a credit squeeze, the bank might not be in a position to renew the credit when it matures, in which case the borrowers might not find alternative resources easily available. To safeguard against that risk, it would be possible to borrow for a term of years at a fixed rate. That rate might be higher in order to make it worth while for the bank to part with its money, or to borrow offsetting medium-term deposits.

The advantage of roll-over credits for borrowers is that in return for an interest rate which includes the spread they can insure the availability of the loan for the entire period for which the money is required. When the spread is narrow – as it is at the time of writing – the market is liable to attract more demand. Considering that the basic rate is an inter-bank interest rate, it is normal that non-banking customers should pay higher rates. This is a natural way to segregate wholesale banking from retail banking.

Given a certain level of liquidity the spread is liable to be affected for individual transactions by the credit rating of the borrowers. The discrepancy between high and low credit rating is apt to narrow down during

periods of high liquidity, because if lenders are keen on lending and there are not enough borrowers of a high credit rating they are more willing to lend to borrowers of a lower credit rating. Conversely, if money is tight, banks do not possess enough resources to meet the full requirements of borrowers with high credit rating and the discrepancy will have to widen considerably before credit is available for borrowers with low credit rating.

The spread is apt to vary even on roll-over credits for the same borrower, according to the extent of its outstanding debt. If the market becomes aware or suspects that a firm has been borrowing excessively, banks become either unwilling to grant it additional roll-over credits or they quote wider spreads. But when banks have a surplus of liquid funds, in a borrowers' market, many of them are inclined to turn a blind eye towards reports of excessive borrowing by firms of high credit rating and prefer to lend to them rather than lending to firms of lower credit rating which have not borrowed excessively. Other banks adhere to their principles of limits for names.

Interest rate prospects are an important factor in determining spreads. If a rise in interest rates is expected, borrowers prefer loans with fixed rates, and may only be prepared to resort to roll-over credits if the spread is narrow. On the other hand if a decline of interest rates is expected, borrowers prefer loans with variable interest rates to those with fixed interest rates, and are prepared to concede higher spreads for roll-over credits. On their part, lenders are prepared to concede narrow spreads when they expect interest rates to rise, rather than forgoing their chances of benefiting from

the rise by lending at fixed rates. Conversely if, rightly or wrongly, they expect interest rates to decline, they want to be compensated for the loss of benefit they would derive by granting loans of fixed interest rates. For this reason spreads should tend to widen during periods when a decline of interest rates is expected. This rule need not operate in practice when high interest rates coincide with a high level of liquidity.

The extent of general risk also influences the spread. In addition to risks involved in lending to borrowers with low credit rating or to those who are borrowing too much, there is a more general risk arising from the possibility of a deterioration of general business conditions. Such a change would mean an increase in the number of insolvencies. When business is bad, insolvencies are not necessarily confined to firms with a low credit rating. In a general depression punctuated with a series of acute crises, such as occurred in the thirties, practically no debtors are considered absolutely safe. The anticipation of some such crisis, or even of some more moderate crises, is apt to induce lenders to abstain from lending in general, and from medium-term lending in particular, unless they are compensated for the higher rise by a wider spread.

There is also an ever-present risk that non-resident debtors might be prevented from meeting their liabilities, not through insolvency, but through the adoption of exchange controls in their countries. The exchange control risk applies to credits in terms of the currency of a third country – such as the dollar – because of the remote possibility that payment might be prevented by exchange control in the United States. Since this would

mean a blocking of non-resident dollar accounts by the American authorities, such an extreme form of exchange control is most unlikely, but it is not impossible.

If the currency of the contract comes under a cloud lenders may expect to be compensated not only for the exchange control risk but also for the risk of a depreciation of the currency in which they lend. Lending in terms of a devaluation-prone currency calls for compensation to lenders in the form of higher interest rates which borrowers should be willing to concede – provided they too hold the view that the currency in question *is* devaluation-prone – because of the benefit they stand to derive from being able to repay their debts in a devalued currency.

Conversely roll-over credits in terms of a revaluation-prone currency offer lenders an opportunity to secure a capital gain as a result of an appreciation of the currency by the time the credit becomes due. For the sake of the chances of such a profit they should be content with a narrower spread and this, together with a lower basic rate of interest on credits in a revaluation-prone currency, might induce some borrowers to assume the risk of loss through a revaluation – always provided that they do not assess that risk too high.

Legal complications that cause difficulties in enforcing claims through action before the Law Courts of the debtor's country constitute a risk for which lenders may be expected to be compensated by insisting on wider spreads. Although a great many contracts contain a clause under which the contract is subject to the laws of the lender's country, when it comes to their enforcement it is impossible to dispense with the co-operation of

the legal authorities of the borrower's country. Above all it is difficult if not impossible to enforce defaulted claims owed or guaranteed by a foreign government or by some institution owned by that government. Gunboat-diplomacy is a matter of the past, and the only incentive for foreign governments to pay up is their desire to borrow again.

This brings us to the risk involved in granting roll-over credits to countries the political stability of which is dubious. There are a great many of them in Latin America, in Africa and in Southern Asia. Even the political stability and solvency of some well-governed countries, such as Iran or Jordan, depend on the life of one individual. Violent changes of régime are apt to be followed by default on, or repudiation of, external liabilities. It is reasonable for lenders to expect compensation for such risk in the form of wider spreads. It is all the more absurd that, even though recent experience is far from having reassured us against such risks, the spread on roll-over credits to countries of dubious stability or solvency or honesty has narrowed considerably during the seventies. While at the beginning of the decade the spread for some of the Latin-American countries was 3 per cent or more, by 1972 it had declined to $1\frac{1}{2}$ per cent or less. The decline of the spread for roll-over credit to Communist-country borrowers to $\frac{3}{4}$ per cent was even more astonishing.

Even in the absence of political upheavals, their mere anticipation is inclined to lead to non-renewals of credits. A wholesale run of creditors is liable to prevent the debtors concerned from meeting their liabilities.

In a great many contracts, the spread is kept down

because the borrowing affiliates are backed up by the parent institution. Until comparatively recently lenders were inclined to assume that debts incurred by affiliates of powerful institutions are covered as a matter of course by the latter's moral guarantee, even in the absence of a legal guarantee in the contract. As a result of recent experience, this is no longer taken for granted.

Lenders now insist on legal guarantees of roll-over credits by governments or government-controlled institutions if the borrowers themselves have not a sufficiently high credit rating, even though it is often a good question to ask 'who guarantees the guarantors?' On the other hand many affiliates of leading banks and multi-national banks controlled jointly by several leading banks are still able to borrow at prime rates even in the absence of any legal guarantees by the banks which own them on the assumption that the banks in question would in all circumstances come to the rescue of their jointly-owned affiliates and of banks in which they are known to hold a substantial minority participation. In one or two instances that assumption proved to have been false.

By and large during 1972 spreads became much too narrow to compensate lenders for the various risks they assumed in granting medium-term credits to borrowers of questionable standing. But it seems to have become much more a matter of prestige for banks to ensure that their names appeared on announcements of syndicated credits. All banks were anxious to 'show the flag', even if, on the basis of the low spreads, roll-over credits became unprofitable. By participating in such transactions they hoped to attract other business from the borrowers

or from other potential borrowers. They hoped that if they participated in roll-over credit syndicates they would be invited also to participate in Euro-issues in company with the names of highly prominent banks.

It is correct to describe roll-over credit transactions undertaken on such terms as 'loss leaders', because of their similarity with the practice of chain stores to sell certain articles at a loss in order to attract other purchasers, who might then also buy other articles once they are on the premises.

The unduly narrow spreads of recent years prevented banks from building up substantial contingency reserves out of which they could cover losses they might suffer through defaults of their debtors. For this reason alone the reduction of spreads as a result of competition of lenders is a matter of some concern. More will be said about this subject in Chapter 14.

CHAPTER SEVEN

Terms of Repayment

The repayment of roll-over credits, as determined by the contract, may take place in one lump sum at the maturity date; or it may take place in several instalments at maturity dates fixed in the contract; or the borrower may have the option to repay the whole or part of the loan on any interest date after the elapse of a minimum period on giving notice as stipulated in the contract. Also situations may arise in which the borrower is entitled to repay the loan, or the lender is entitled to reclaim the loan, before maturity, in circumstances in which the possibility of such repayments is provided for in the contract.

Under many contracts the borrower is entitled to the use of the money loaned to him right up to the final maturity date. Other contracts provide for the repayment of the amount borrowed in fixed instalments maturing on fixed dates. In some instances part repayment is to be made on each interest date, and occasionally the sinking-fund formula is applied under which the fixed amounts payable on interest dates include a declining adaptable interest element and an increasing capital element. More often less frequent repayments of larger amounts are provided for by the contract.

Terms of Repayment

Many contracts determine a minimum limit and a maximum limit for the period during which the debtor has to repay the credit, but within those limits the actual date or dates may be determined by the debtor, subject to such notice as is stipulated in the contract. This option of early repayments is a great advantage to the borrower, not only because he need not continue to pay interest on the loan when the money is no longer required, but also because it provides him with an opportunity for taking advantage of any cheaper facilities that might become available before the date of maturity – or dates of maturities – fixed in the contract.

During a period of rising interest rates, when under the terms of a roll-over credit the borrower has to pay higher and higher interest rates in accordance with the higher rates quoted in the market on interest dates, an early repayment option enables him to terminate the loan if it ceases to be profitable for him to continue to use the money at such a high cost. Some contracts contain a provision under which the borrower is entitled to repay the credit if and when the interest rate rises to a certain level. But many more contracts grant him an option of early repayment which is independent of the level of interest rates.

During a period of declining interest rates roll-over credits give borrowers the full benefits derived from the decline of interest rates in the market of the Euro-currency in terms of which the credit is fixed. Situations are apt to arise, however, in which it becomes less costly for the borrower to cover his credit requirements in some other form. An early repayment option enables him to

take full advantage of such opportunities. When money becomes easier increased competition of lenders, too, might enable borrowers to obtain roll-over credits on more favourable terms than those which were available to him at the time of the conclusion of the contract, provided that the contract contains an early repayment clause. Even during periods of rising interest rates and tightening money, borrowers expecting a further rise might consider it to be to their advantage to finance their requirements through capital issues or through other alternative methods.

As a general rule lenders have no option to demand early repayment except in special circumstances (to be discussed below). If lenders had the right to demand early repayment borrowers would lose the advantage derived from medium-term borrowing. Debtors might be called upon to repay their debts at a time when they might find it difficult or impossible to raise the necessary cash, or when they might only be able to do so on less favourable terms. If debtors exercise their options of early repayment it is true that lenders might find it difficult to re-employ the money on equally profitable terms. But banks are always able to find a market in which they could employ the funds, even though during periods of declining interest rates and increasing liquidity they might have to do so on less advantageous terms than those obtained even after the downward adjustment of the interest rates on roll-over credits. It is for this reason that the spread on roll-over credits with a one-way option to the borrower's benefit is wider than on credits without such options. Alternatively lenders in a borrowers' market may offer such an option as an

additional inducement when competing for the business against their rivals.

If the practice of giving lenders the option to recall their credits were widespread it would go a long way towards discouraging borrowers from availing themselves of roll-over credit facilities, owing to the uncertainty to which they would be exposed. On the other hand one-sided options in favour of borrowers are widely practised without discouraging participation in such operations by lenders, because lenders are in a better position than borrowers to cope with the situation arising from an early termination of a medium-term credit contract.

Most contracts stipulate that if borrowers make use of their early repayment options then repayment must take place at interest dates, though some lenders have no objections to broken interest periods that would occur if repayment was made on other dates. Early repayments usually have to be made in round amounts. In many contracts it is stipulated that the repayments must be a minimum amount or its multiples. Frequent repayments of varying amounts would involve everyone concerned in much additional clerical work.

Borrowers have to give the agents due notice of their decision to exercise their early repayment option. The most frequently fixed period is thirty days, though the contracts may fix longer or shorter periods. There are instances of contracts that fix a longer notice during the early period of the loan and shorter notice during a later period. In given circumstances the borrower may approach the lender with the request to forgo part of the notice to which the latter is entitled under the

contract. Since banks are anxious to ensure the goodwill of the borrower and are anxious to acquire a reputation for being obliging to borrowers instead of insisting on the letter of the contract, early repayment without the full contractual notice is usually conceded.

Under some contracts which do not have a repayment option clause the borrower is entitled to repay the loan if the adjusted interest rate exceeds a certain figure. Occasionally the lender is entitled to claim repayment if the adjusted interest rate declines below a certain figure. As this only occurs amidst easy monetary conditions the borrower does not suffer undue inconvenience if the lender exercises that option, for the chances are that he would not find it difficult to raise alternative credit facilities.

But both from the point of view of lenders and from that of borrowers it is always inconvenient to have to negotiate another loan contract because the other party has exercised its early repayment option. Such negotiations always involve delays and expense. Under some contracts the party that makes use of his option has to pay a fixed sum to cover expenses, or he has to pay a penalty of $\frac{1}{8}$ per cent or such other penalty as may be fixed in the contract.

Roll-over credit contracts often contain provisions for repayment if the situation is changed as a result of new exchange control measures, new taxation measures, or new measures providing for reserve requirements. In the event of default on an interest payment or capital repayment the whole amount of the credits becomes immediately due for repayment. Defaulters are also penalised by an obligation to pay higher interest rates

which are fixed in the contract. Independently of any provisions for early repayment, most contracts contain an option authorising borrowers not to draw the full amount of the loan.

Notice of the borrower's decision to avail himself of the option of early repayment is given to the agent who communicates it to the managing banks.

CHAPTER EIGHT

Currency Options

Most roll-over credits are in dollars, and the funds are usually provided out of the general pool of the Euro-dollar market. But similar credits may also be fixed in Deutschemarks, or in sterling (for U.K. borrowers), or in other leading currencies. Some contracts give the borrower the option to borrow in one of several currencies or in composite monetary units or in some composite monetary account.

Many contracts are drawn up which entitle the borrowers to choose from among several currencies the one in which they require the first or a later instalment of the loan to be paid, or in which they may draw the entire credit. The borrower must inform the agent of his choice of currency and must give him notice the length of which is prescribed in the contract. The minimum notice is often five days. Since all participating banks have to decide whether the borrower's choice of currency is acceptable to them, a five days' notice is not unreasonable.

Contracts usually contain a reservation under which the lender banks are entitled to refuse to accept the borrower's choice of the denomination of the loan or of any of its instalments if the currency chosen by him is not easily available at a reasonable price. Of course in theory

all major currencies are supposed to be available in a good market at a reasonable price. In practice exchange control might make it difficult for the lenders to comply with the borrower's wish. Or it might become abnormally costly to acquire the currency in question as a result of a squeeze in the market or of other changes that may have occurred since the conclusion of the credit.

Repayment is always due to be made in the same currency in which the credit, or any of its instalments, was made available to the borrower; interest, too, is due in the same currency. If in spite of this condition borrowers prefer to choose a particular currency the reason is usually because they expect the currency to depreciate before the credit is repaid. There are obvious advantages in borrowing in a devaluation-prone or depreciation-prone currency. But in many instances, if devaluation or depreciation of the particular currency appears to be imminent, the authorities concerned are liable to resort to measures which make it difficult for the lenders to procure the currency in question or, if for some reason the borrower should choose a scarce currency, the lender would only be able to acquire it at an abnormally high price. Some contracts contain provisions to safeguard lenders against consequences of changes in parities between the conclusion of the contract and its implementation.

Some contracts contain provisions authorising the borrower to convert the loan into some other currency on any interest date. But the reservations referred to above also apply to such options.

If the currency chosen by the borrower is not acceptable to the lenders then they, the lenders, are entitled

under many contracts to lend dollars. Sometimes contracts rule that unless all participating banks agree to the currency chosen by the borrower the contract will be cancelled. But usually the borrower is given the option to accept the credit in dollars.

If the amount of the credit is fixed in dollars and the borrower exercises his option to be paid in some other currency, the equivalent amount is reckoned on the basis of the mean rate of the non-dollar currency in terms of dollars quoted by the IMF two days before the relevant date. Under some contracts, if no mean rate is quoted in that currency by the IMF on the relevant date, the amount is then reckoned on the basis of the offered rate of that currency in the London foreign exchange market.

If the borrower chooses payment in dollars then under most contracts or in the absence of any provision to the contrary, the lenders have to accept his choice of currency. Likewise, if the lenders notify the borrowers through their agent that they intend to pay in dollars, then, in the absence of a provision in the contract to the contrary, the borrower has to accept it, although under some contracts he would have the option of cancelling the deal.

Should a change occur after the notice of the choice of the currency has been received then, under some contracts, the lenders may notify the borrower not later than at 10 a.m., two business days before the date of payment, that they wish to change the currency. The borrower will then notify the agents as to whether he is willing to accept the lenders' decision or prefers to cancel the deal.

Currency Options

One of the many terms of roll-over credits which could and should be clarified is the exact meaning of the changes which justify refusal to accept the borrowers' choice of currency. In some contracts they are defined very broadly as changes in the national or international financial, political or economic conditions, or in the exchange rate, or in exchange control 'as would in the opinion of the managing bank make it impracticable for any drawing to be made in the currency concerned or for any borrowing to be converted into a currency other than the dollar'. Such broad definition empowers the lenders to veto the choice of currency if they so wish, and thereby invalidate for all practical purposes the currency option included in the contract. The only safeguard for borrowers is to deal exclusively with lenders whose standing is first class, who have a reputation for fair dealing and who would not wish to risk their reputation unless there was some very well-founded reason for refusing to accept the choice of the borrowers.

If any change in the exchange rate should be regarded as an adequate reason for vetoing the borrower's choice then the inclusion of the currency option would become entirely pointless, for any change which would make it worthwhile for the borrower to choose a certain currency in preference to others would necessarily be against the lenders' interests. To be more exact, the chances are that any reason for which the borrower would consider it to be to his advantage to receive the loan in a certain currency would be considered by the lenders to be a reason for preferring not to grant the loan in that currency.

Under a genuine currency option clause the borrower

should be entitled to choose any of the currencies named in the contract, always assuming that only currencies which are freely convertible into each other by nonresident holders are named therein. Only new measures of exchange control or official policies aimed at tightening the market in the currency concerned should be acceptable justification for vetoing a currency named in the contract.

The problem of currency option that the borrower could exercise in respect of later drawings on the credit, providing for a conversion of the currency on any interest date, is even more difficult to solve. The longer the time lag between the conclusion of the contract and the moment when the borrower wishes to exercise his option the more there is a likelihood of a change in the situation. The extent of the advantages of choosing one particular non-dollar currency would be liable to increase from the borrower's point of view and so would the extent of the disadvantages that the acceptance of his choice would be liable to entail to the lenders.

The extent of potential advantages and disadvantages is greatly increased when the currencies involved are floating or when the government concerned pursues a policy of frequent changes of parities. But then there would be a risk involved even in borrowing in dollars, given the possibility of changes in the dollar's parities and of changes in the gold parities of the borrower's currency. Indeed amidst the prevailing unsettled stage of exchange rates, hardly any international credit transaction with a currency option can be free of exchange risk.

CHAPTER NINE

The Secondary Market

An enquiry into any comparatively new market seldom produces a unanimous answer. Those who are actively engaged in the market possess first-hand knowledge about the part of the market in which they are engaged, but very few of them are equally familiar with the working of the entire market. There is usually disagreement, not only about the interpretation of the relevant facts, but even about the facts themselves. But in no previous instance have I encountered such utter lack of unanimity as in my enquiries into the secondary market in roll-over credits.

At the one extreme, many bankers told me that there was no such thing as a secondary market in roll-over credits. At the other extreme, I was given to understand that in certain types of notes, at any rate, there was quite an active secondary market, in which any lender was in a position to dispose of his notes. This striking difference of opinion is, perhaps, simply explained by the fact that those bankers who denied the existence of a secondary market had never had any dealings in it and therefore they thought fit to ignore its very existence, while those who affirm the existence of such a market specialised in such operations. On the

basis of their respective experiences, they presented two totally different pictures of the same subject.

Needless to say, roll-over credits granted by banks to their own clients have no secondary markets. If, however, the amount involved is large, the lending bank is in a position to dispose of part of it by issuing Participation Certificates. When they are issued simultaneously with the granting of the credit they constitute the primary market. But if they are issued later they form a kind of secondary market in which the original lender can unload that part of his claim which he does not want to carry till maturity.

The Participation Certificates themselves may or may not have a secondary market. In the majority of instances the existence of such a market is not essential from the holder's point of view, because the banks issuing the certificates are usually prepared to repurchase them. There is no legal obligation on the banks' part to do so, neither is there even a moral obligation. But in normal circumstances issuing banks are willing to repurchase their certificates at the current interest rates, plus a spread which is somewhat wider than it was when the certificate was issued. It is to their interest to do so in order to create goodwill, which will make it easier for them to place certificates on future occasions. Such certificates are usually not transferable, so that holders depend on the willingness of the issuing banks to repurchase them.

Notes issued on behalf of the borrowers are very often transferable and in many contracts it is stipulated that their transfer requires the managing bank's consent but, generally speaking, such consent is seldom withheld. In

other contracts the holders of the notes simply have to notify the managing bank about the change in ownership. Sometimes the buyers of the notes state in the contract that it is not their present intention to transfer the notes. This implies that transfers are not encouraged, but are not prevented, for holders are entitled to change their minds. Occasionally there is a provision in the contract which precludes the sale of the notes in certain countries, such as the United States and Canada. Such provisions do not prevent the development of a secondary market, but their presence in the contract naturally limits it.

In the majority of instances in which a secondary market exists the rates are often a matter of negotiation. This does not prevent, however, speculative operations. Buyers may speculate on the decline in Euro-dollar rates or in other rates which determine the rates for notes in the secondary market, or on a contraction of the spread. Sellers may speculate on the rise in interest rates or on a widening of the spread. If, however, there are no two-way quotations, speculators have no means of knowing what they stand to lose on the turn. The rates and spreads would have to move appreciably in their favour before they could make a profit that would make it worth their while to undertake the risk involved.

Usually only large issues of notes have a reasonably good secondary market. The managing banks see to it that such a market does develop. To encourage it they, or associated houses, make two-way quotations. In some instances, notes are listed in the Luxembourg stock exchange. In some notes there is from time to time quite

an active turnover, though of course it bears no comparison with the turnover in the secondary market for Euro-issues.

Some managing banks realise the importance of developing a secondary market in roll-over credits for the sake of assisting the primary market. It is not enough if participants in the credits depend on the willingness of managing banks to repurchase the notes. Apart from anything else, lending-banks of standing may not like to avail themselves of such favours because, if they asked the managing bank to refund their money, it would disclose the fact that they were short of cash. Some banks do not consider it very dignified to make use of such facilities and they would not do so unless they were in a tight corner. It is certainly not practised as a matter of routine, and there is always the risk that should money become really tight, the managing banks themselves would prefer not to return the money in the absence of any obligation on their part to do so.

One of the advantages of a good secondary market is that it is possible to deal in the notes between interest dates. Such transactions involve some complications, because neither party is in a position to know the rate which will be fixed on the next interest date for the next interest period.

It is particularly important to have a secondary market in notes maturing in more than seven years, because it is not always easy to negotiate offsetting deposits for periods of, say, ten years or more.

A high proportion of the buyers in the secondary market consists of American or Swiss banks, the latter acting usually for American or other non-Swiss clients.

London usually plays the part of the entrepôt. It neither borrows nor buys on the U.K. account on the secondary market any notes in terms of foreign currencies.

Differentials between rates in the primary and secondary markets are affected by the general conditions of liquidity. When money is plentiful, most holders are not keen on selling, and they will not do so unless they get rates which differ very slightly from the rates at which issues are made in the primary market. If money is tight, many holders are anxious to sell and are willing to do so on less favourable conditions. Differentials are affected by the trend of the interest rates and of the spread. If spreads tend to narrow, the issuing banks may be willing to repurchase the notes on the original terms.

Even though some notes have good secondary markets, generally speaking the secondary markets leave much to be desired. There is ample scope for an improvement of the system. Of course only large issues stand a chance of ever developing a good secondary market. But then small roll-over credits can usually be handled by the bank concerned and need not have even a primary market, let alone a secondary market. On the other hand there is no reason why really large issues of roll-over notes for five years and longer should not have a good secondary market, in which case they would be in a position to compete with short Euro-bonds.

CHAPTER TEN

The Boom in Roll-Over Credits

The increase in roll-over credits in the early seventies has been one of the outstanding success stories in the sphere of international finance; comparable with the success stories of Euro-dollars, Euro-bonds, CDs and inter-bank deposits. The extent of its expansion cannot be quantified, because only large credits are publicised, and even those are not necessarily given publicity. Most small roll-over credits and some large ones are a matter of private arrangements between banks and their customers. The fact that only the larger transactions are publicised does not justify the assumption that small borrowers do not use roll-over credits. They have the same reasons for asking their banks for credits with adjustable interest rates as large borrowers, and the banks have no reason for refusing to accommodate them. Possibly the terms are costlier for small clients, but the same is true for all forms of credits, not only because the credit ratings of small firms are usually lower than those of big firms, but also because the handling of a large number of small accounts involves more clerical labour than the handling of a small number of big accounts.

The reason why banks may be less keen on granting a large number of small roll-over credits than they

are on granting a smaller number of big roll-over credits is, in addition to clerical labour, that hedging against the former is somewhat more difficult than against the latter. A big transaction can be hedged against by borrowing a corresponding inter-bank deposit for the same period and in the same currency, or in a different currency with the exchange risk covered. A multitude of small roll-over credits maturing on a variety of dates would have to be covered by a number of offsetting time deposits. But the maturity of such deposits could not be synchronised with those of the credits.

The granting of medium-term credits – whether with fixed interest rates or with variable interest rates – out of the proceeds of deposits at sight or at short notice, or even out of the proceeds of time deposits maturing at shorter dates, involves a certain amount of risk. However, commercial banks with a large turnover usually rely on the law of averages and assume that changes in the multitude of small accounts will offset each other more or less or, if there is a discrepancy, the banks may rely on covering it in the inter-bank market which is the clearing house of the surpluses and deficiencies of banks, in addition to the clearing house of the traditional money market.

The expansion of roll-over credits is partly a normal institutional change. Whenever some new device or new facility is introduced its use tends to become increasingly popular. An increasing number of borrowers and lenders discover the new device or extend its use. The resulting increase of its use continues until it has reached the saturation point on the basis of prevailing business conditions. Any further increase would depend on business

expansion. Of course there is always a possibility that full institutional expansion would not be reached for some time, and anyhow it is difficult to draw the border-line between institutional expansion and expansion through other causes.

As far as lenders were concerned the increase of the use of the new device was stimulated by the availability of Euro-dollars owing to the decline of their use by American, Japanese, German and other borrowers. Ever since the emergence of the Euro-dollar system it found new uses again and again whenever its previous use declined. Its latest use is for the purpose of financing roll-over credits or of serving as offsetting deposits to lenders. Precisely because banks were unable to use their Euro-dollars mainly for the purposes for which they had been used extensively until about the beginning of the seventies, they became keen on granting roll-over credits even in the face of greatly reduced profit-margins which were operating as a result of the decline of spreads.

Euro-dollars are not the only form in which the increase of roll-over credits has been financed. There has been an increase in sterling CDs and London dollar CDs, and the proceeds of the funds thus raised have been largely used for increasing the amount of roll-over credits. Similarly deposits borrowed in the inter-bank sterling market have been largely used for granting roll-over credits to domestic borrowers in sterling.

It is always difficult to say with any degree of certainty whether in this sphere the first chicken preceded the first egg. Possibly in many instances the initiative for the expansion came from the increase in the volume of deposits that banks were able to use as offsetting

deposits, and it was the availability of the liquid resources thus raised that induced them to go out of their way to expand their roll-over credits. In other instances it was the increase in the demand for roll-over credits that induced the banks to raise the necessary funds by borrowing in the various markets. The repayment of large amounts of Euro-dollars by borrowers must have stimulated potential lenders of roll-over credits to increase their commitments. They not only satisfied the demand initiated by borrowers but went out of their way to take the initiative to find eligible borrowers. In many instances when borrowers were reluctant to commit themselves to pay the prevailing high interest rates on fixed interest credits it was the banks who suggested to them the alternative method that would enable them to benefit by a subsequent decline in interest rates.

It seems probable that, had the heavy borrowing of Euro-dollars for various fixed maturities or in the form of deposits subject to notice continued, there would not have been so much liquid funds available for lending in the form of roll-over credits. Nor would there have been so much demand for such facilities if, following on the decline of interest rates in the early seventies, they had not risen once more to levels at which borrowers became reluctant to commit themselves to the prevailing high interest rates for medium-term credits.

In any case, as a result of the efforts made by a number of Governments to check inflation by means of credit squeezes, the resulting deflationary unemployment induced most of them to reverse their policies. By 1972 the volume of liquid resources increased very considerably

in advanced countries, and this alone came to provide a strong incentive for banks to make profitable use of their resources. As explained in previous chapters, the demand for medium-term credits increased because of the growing requirements of capital goods and because of the increasing practice of adopting long production programmes.

But the most important direct cause of the boom in roll-over credits was the fierce competition between banks. For the sake of increasing their volume of roll-over credits, many of them departed from well-established traditions of prudent banking. It is of course always easy for banks to expand their business if they are prepared to accommodate borrowers with a lower credit rating. The large number of new banks, anxious to secure clients, and the determination of well-established banks not to lose ground, between them brought about a considerable increase in the turnover.

The willingness of banks to lend to borrowers with a lower credit rating was explained partly by the relatively low level of business failures. Non-stop inflation is apt to reduce the number of insolvencies, because with rising prices it is easier to sell at a profit. The difference between good judgement and mistaken judgement on the part of manufacturers and merchants in deciding what to produce or buy is in such a stituation merely that bad judgement means smaller profits and a slower turnover. The judgement has to be particularly bad before it leads to actual losses and the accumulation of frozen stocks, to a sufficient extent to cause insolvency – in spite of the rising demand and the rising trend of prices.

The Boom in Roll-Over Credits

High interest rates slow down the velocity of money, because everybody tries to delay the payment of liabilities as long as possible in order to save interest charges. This was an additional reason for the increased demand for medium-term credits to tide over producers and merchants until they succeeded in collecting their overdue claims. The possibility of a decline in interest rates after their spectacular rise made it appear expedient for borrowers to use credits with variable interest rates, rather than conventional credits with fixed interest rates.

The spectacular expansion in the volume of roll-over credits and in other forms of medium-term credits recalls the lending boom of the late twenties, when in large or even medium-sized German towns it was almost impossible for visitors to find accommodation in first-class hotels because they were full of representatives of foreign banks anxious to persuade municipal authorities, public utility enterprises and other potential borrowers to borrow through their respective banks. As a result of the lenders' competition, the borrowers were able to raise all the funds they needed – in fact rather more than they really needed – on rather generous terms. The end of the story was general default. It is to be hoped that this history will not repeat itself in respect of the roll-over credit boom.

It may appear strange to the layman that the boom in roll-over credits did not reduce itself to absurdity before it came to assume such striking proportions. After all if the level of interest rates is considered to be too high and is expected to decline, lenders are liable to become as keen on insisting on fixed high rates as borrowers are on

insisting on adjustable rates. On the face of it, this should mean a deadlock. But lenders are in a position to hedge against losses through a decline in interest rates by re-borrowing in the market the amount they lend in the form of roll-over credits. Furthermore all people in the financial world do not hold identical opinions about the prospects of interest rates. Even if they are high they might well rise even higher before they begin to decline. Many lenders are prepared to engage in roll-over credit transactions without hedging against a fall in interest rates, because they do not expect a fall in interest rates for some time to come. During the four years beginning with the spring of 1969 the trend of interest rates changed several times, and on balance the rises exceeded anticipations considerably. That experience is liable to repeat itself, especially if, as seems probable, inflation continues, and if the market should become increasingly inflation-conscious. In any case, should the trend turn downward, lenders would be in a position to hedge.

CHAPTER ELEVEN

Effect on Growth

Until recently, economic expansion was handicapped to no slight degree by an inadequacy of medium-term credit facilities. In the absence of such facilities, business firms had to choose between raising unduly large share and debenture capital, or depending on being able to obtain repeated renewals of short-term bank credits. As a result of the increase of prosperity during the fifties and sixties, and of the increase in the demand for capital goods, the requirements of medium-term credits increased considerably. The market for capital issues might have been unable to meet those requirements in full if it had not been supplanted by the development of medium-term bank credits.

Had it not been for the availability of such credit facilities, business expansion would have been handicapped for lack of capital. The market for long-term issues would not have been able to cover all the requirements created by new inventions of capital goods, such as for instance costly computers. It would have been difficult, in the absence of medium-term credit facilities, to finance new methods of transport, involving the purchase of super-tankers, transport planes, giant airliners, container ships, etc.

Presumably the progress represented by the increasing use of such capital goods could have been achieved also in the absence of roll-over credits. But had it not been for the adoption of that device and the rapid expansion of its use, progress would have been handicapped. Even though many roll-over credit transactions simply replaced financing by means of repeatedly renewed short-term credits or capital issues, much of the billions of dollars borrowed by that device was additional to other forms of raising funds. Admittedly investment demand for equities and for convertible bonds for the purpose of hedging against inflation was on the increase. But it might not have been sufficient to provide all the money needed for medium-term credit.

It is, therefore, reasonable to claim that roll-over credits have contributed to no slight degree towards the escalation of economic growth during the sixties and the seventies. In particular after the reversal of the credit squeeze at the beginning of the seventies, the re-expansion in the volume of bank credits assumed to no slight degree the form of increase in roll-over credits. It was largely because of the extensive use of this device that the volume of bank credits rose above the peak it attained prior to its reduction during the squeeze.

Roll-over credits greatly assisted the economic expansion of developing countries which would not have been in a position to raise capital through public issues. Although they received various forms of foreign aid, their credit rating was too low for attracting private investors; they had to depend on loans from the World Bank

and credits guaranteed by the Governments of the lending countries. Strangely enough banks which would not have lent their names to public issues of such countries – issues which were to be taken up by private investors – were prepared to lend them their own money, and that of their depositors, in the form of roll-over credits.

Whatever one may think of such transactions from the point of view of conservative banking, they certainly assisted in making for a better utilisation of the economic resources of developing countries. They helped to increase the output of their primary products, and they also assisted in the industrialisation of these countries to some degree. Thus roll-over credits went some way towards raising the standard of living in 'have-not' countries, and they assisted in the international redistribution of wealth and income.

In advanced countries, too, roll-over credits must have contributed to no slight degree towards the increase in the rate of productivity and of the actual output of goods and services. They helped industries to be more independent on the ups and downs of monetary policy. For even though from time to time credit squeezes prevented banks from expanding their roll-over credits as well as other forms of bank credits, once the borrower obtained a roll-over credit for five years, seven years or even longer, the lender was unable to cancel his credit in spite of a credit squeeze.

This did not necessarily mean, however, that the business community as a whole obtained more bank credit during periods of credit squeeze. If the monetary authorities fixed a ceiling for bank lendings and if the banks were unable to call up the loans they had made in

the form of roll-over credits, it meant that they had to call up other credits which they had lent to other borrowers for short periods or which were subject to short notice. During such periods, current market rates increased, which meant that roll-over credits were renewed on interest dates at higher rates. But when money was easy borrowers whose contracts contained an early repayment option were in a position to repay roll-over credits before their final maturity date.

Allowing for all the above considerations there can be no doubt that roll-over credits have made their contribution towards accelerated growth. The question is, are we entitled to consider growth an unmitigated blessing? We must bear in mind that it has contributed towards increased pollution and towards the aggravation of other disadvantages of growth on the environment. It has also been responsible to a considerable extent for the progress of inflation and its resulting demoralising effect on the nation.

What is more, as a result of accelerated economic growth, the economic system of the free world has become more vulnerable. There is now an increased risk of grave economic setbacks and of major financial crises. It may well be asked whether a slower rate of growth in the absence of large-scale use of roll-over credits would not have been more in accordance with the basic interests of mankind in the long run. In a world suffering from growth-hysteria this point of view is not likely to receive much attention. Yet it is well worth considering that possibly in the absence of roll-over credits there might have been a better chance for interrupting periods of growth by much-needed periods of consolidation.

Effect on Growth

One aspect of the impact of growth on monetary trend which has not received sufficient attention is that growth is inherently inflationary because, among other reasons, of the time-lag between the input and the output. All increase of input assumes the form of additional consumer purchasing power. It takes some time before the additional purchasing power created by the additional input is offset by the additional supplies of goods and services created as a result of the growth. In any case growth entails not only the production of goods and services which become available to consumers but also increased expenditure on roads, schools, hospitals, etc., which does not absorb the additional purchasing power created by the increased input. But even if we were to assume for the sake of argument that growth consists entirely of additional output of goods and services available to consumers, we must bear in mind the time-lag during which the additional purchasing power tends to cause an increase of prices. This increase is stepped up by the multiplier effect and the accelerator effect of the additional consumer purchasing power. By the time the output reaches the markets it would only offset part of the additional purchasing power created by the input, and it would only reverse part of the inflationary effect. If growth is more or less continuous its inflationary effect is never reversed or even halted.

For this reason alone and apart altogether from their other inflationary effects which will be discussed in the next chapter, economic growth created by an expansion of roll-over credits is inherently inflationary. In this respect there is no difference, however, between econo-

mic growth due to expansion of roll-over credits and to other methods of increasing the volume of credit. Roll-over credits are only specifically inflationary to the extent to which they are in addition to the expansion of credit brought about by other means of increasing the volume of money.

CHAPTER TWELVE

Is it Inflation?

As we repeatedly pointed out, to some extent roll-over credits have merely replaced alternative borrowing facilities, especially short-term credits, medium-term credits at fixed interest rates, and capital issues. At first sight it might seem obvious that to the extent to which this was the case the new device has not added to the total volume of bank credits and is therefore not one of the causes of inflation. Even if we were to concede this without argument, there would remain the amounts of roll-over credits which are additional to other forms of credits. There is every reason to believe that the application of this new method has in fact added to the grand total of the volume of money.

Even though roll-over credits are often used for financing long production programmes which are applied to consumer goods and capital goods alike – that is to say they are used for ascertaining that the financial facilities will be available as and when needed over a long period to cover the requirements of planned production – their main purpose is to finance the production of, and the trade in, capital goods. To the extent to which the increase in the amount of roll-over credits means a decline in the amount of short-term credits

used for financing consumer goods, it tends to reduce the volume of goods available to meet consumers' purchasing power.

If we accept Dalton's simple definition – presumably inspired by Keynes – according to which inflation is a state of affairs in which 'too much money is chasing too few goods', any increase in the production and supplies of capital goods at the cost of reducing the output and supply of consumer goods must be essentially inflationary. It is the supply–demand relationship of consumer goods that determines the trend of the cost of living in the short run. Admittedly in the long run the increase in the supply of capital goods would react favourably on the supply of consumer goods. But as Keynes remarked, in the long run we are all dead. The immediate effect of diverting credit resources from short-term credits to roll-over credits – unless it is for the purposes of long production programmes of consumer goods – is a rise in the price of consumer goods. Such a rise can become self-aggravating and it is liable to proceed very far before the increase in the supply of capital goods begins to produce its effect on the volume and prices of consumer goods.

The inflationary effect of the industrial revolution of the U.S.S.R. since the war shows that even in a 'centralised economy' economic laws cannot be altogether controlled. Because a very high proportion of the Soviet Union's productive capacity is diverted from the production of consumer goods to the production of capital goods – in addition to the proportion diverted to be used for arms production and for the exploration of the Outer Space – prices in the Soviet Union have risen to an

extent comparable to their rise in Capitalist countries. In spite of the complete domination of trade unions by the Communist State the diversion of productive capacity from consumer goods to capital goods could not be prevented from producing its inflationary effect.

Nor could inflation be prevented in Japan, which country experienced the most spectacular industrial revolution in economic history. The 'spirit of Nippon' has failed to prevent rapid industrialisation from producing an inflationary effect. No matter how hard and how efficiently the Japanese worker may work, the diversion of a high proportion of his working capacity from the production of consumer goods for the domestic market to the production of capital goods has generated inflation.

Assuming that the use of roll-over credits has left the total volume of money unchanged, the question is, how is it likely to affect the velocity of circulation of money? Short-term credits used for financing the production and sale of consumer goods are self-liquidating, so that the increase in the volume of credit created when granting such credits is cancelled out when they mature. On the other hand roll-over credits, like other medium-term credits, are not repayable for some years, so that the purchasing power they create is not cancelled out for years.

Increase of production, whether of consumer goods or capital goods, means an increase of wage-earners' purchasing power. When consumer goods are produced their increased supplies offset that additional supply of consumer purchasing power. But when capital goods are produced the surplus purchasing power is not

cancelled out for a long time to come. Meanwhile the increased expenditure produces its multiplier and accelerator effect.

However, it seems highly probable that the use of roll-over credits does increase the volume of money. It tends to increase the volume of Euro-dollars, because the additional demand for them tends to increase their rates, which again attracts additional supplies of dollars. Part of the proceeds of roll-over credits is re-deposited with banks by their recipients – the borrowers or those who are paid for their goods and services by the borrowers out of the proceeds of roll-over credits – so that the volume of deposits is increased. Since the debt created is not repaid for a long time, the purchasing power it creates is exercised again and again. In addition to its direct initial effect, it produces its multiplier effect and also its accelerator effect. Capital expenditure stimulates consumption and the resulting consumer expenditure stimulates capital expenditure.

Of course it is impossible to guesstimate, even approximately, the inflationary effect of roll-over credits. Many of the roll-over credits are never publicised and cannot be quantified. Their multiplier and accelerator effects are incalculable.

The next question to be answered is, what happens if roll-over credits are used instead of long-term issues? Such long-term issues are taken up by investors who thereby relinquish the use of their purchasing power for a long period. On the other hand the certificates issued in connection with roll-over credits are taken up by banks and by institutional investors which would not use their purchasing power for the acquisition of consumer

goods. The issue of bonds is more likely to reduce consumer demand than the granting of roll-over credits.

The contrary is in fact the case. In all probability roll-over credits increase not only the volume of bank money but also the volume of consumer demand. Their availability increases the total demand for credits, and many borrowers who would be unwilling to borrow at unduly high fixed interest rates are willing to borrow if they have a chance to benefit by a fall in interest rates.

On the other hand during periods of credit squeezes banks are apt to be reluctant to grant roll-over credits, because these medium-term credits could not be recalled if the total of their outstanding credit exceeds the authorised ceiling, or if they find it difficult to comply with reserve requirements. It is much easier to call short-term credits. But for that very reason many borrowers prefer roll-over credits, especially when a credit squeeze is threatening.

Precisely because roll-over credits are not self-liquidating in the short run, they are liable to create a lasting inflationary effect. They are likely to inspire confidence in the business community, because the lenders are not in a position to cancel their credits for a number of years. For this reason the borrowers are likely to spend the proceeds more freely on capital goods, and they thereby encourage the production of capital goods instead of consumer goods. To the extent to which this is done so does the volume of consumer purchasing power increase without a corresponding increase in the volume of consumer goods.

Another reason why the expansion of roll-over credits is inflationary is the keen competition among lenders.

There is of course also competition in traditional forms of lending, but competition is not nearly as keen as it is in respect of some new form of lending. Thus there was, and still is, more competition among lenders of Euro-currencies than among banks granting conventional forms of credits. As we shall see in Chapter 14 the extent of the expansion of roll-over credits is causing concern in official circles.

There can be little doubt that the appearance and expansion of this new device have contributed towards the escalation of inflation to no slight degree. In so far as banks have been over-lending the risk of a crisis has increased, in addition to the adverse effect of the resulting steep rise in prices.

CHAPTER THIRTEEN

Impact on Foreign Exchanges

All credits granted in terms of a foreign currency – that is, in a currency that is not the local currency either of the lender or of a borrower – are liable to affect the foreign exchange market. A similar effect is liable to be produced if the lender lends in terms of the borrower's currency, or if the borrower borrows in terms of the lender's currency.

(1) If a lender lends in a currency other than his own, he may buy the necessary foreign exchange.

(2) The borrower may convert the proceeds of the credit into his own currency or into a third currency, to meet his requirements.

(3) The borrower may sell the proceeds in order to create a short position in the currency he borrowed.

(4) The lender or the borrower may cover the exchange risk on the amount lent or borrowed.

(5) Maturing foreign exchange contracts may be settled by means of borrowing the currency required instead of buying it (negative effect).

(6) Maturing Euro-currency contracts may be settled by borrowing the required currency instead of buying it (negative effect).

(7) Borrowers may buy the amounts required for the payment of principal and interest.

All this effect may be produced by any form of international credit transaction. The only circumstance in which roll-over credits actually increase the volume of foreign exchange operations is when it is in addition to other forms of international credit transactions instead of merely replacing them. Such a situation does arise, so that it is reasonable to conclude that the adoption and expansion of the roll-over credits system tend to cause an expansion of activity in the foreign exchange market, in addition to causing an expansion of activity in the Euro-currency market.

Roll-over credits are liable to affect forward exchanges to a higher degree than spot exchanges. Since the interest period in most contracts is six months, both lenders and borrowers may want to hedge for that period, not only against the interest risk rate—but also against the exchange risk. Of course they now have facilities at their disposal to cover the exchange risk right up to maturity – it is possible to negotiate forward transactions for anything up to five years or more. But the exchange risk for such long periods can be covered with the aid of a medium-term Euro-currency transaction, always provided that the parties concerned expect interest rates to move in their favour.

In given circumstances an expansion of roll-over credits gives rise to a substantial increase of forward transactions. In addition to affecting the forward rate this tends to affect the spot rate as well, that is if the transactions assume the form of swap transactions. In addition to their direct effect on the reserves, the re-

sulting pressure is apt to affect the reserves indirectly.

Although in theory roll-over credits are only supposed to affect the Euro-currency rates concerned, in practice interest rates in other currencies and in other centres are also liable to be affected. This again tends to react on exchange rates, both spot and especially forward.

A much more direct effect of roll-over credits on exchange rates is through its influence on imports and exports. Roll-over credits are often tied credits, enabling the borrower to import from the lending country instead of importing from some other country. Even if no such condition is attached to the loan it is more than possible that the lender's country attracts a high proportion of the amount lent. If large amounts are at stake it is obviously in the interest of the borrowers to spend the proceeds in the lending country, for an improvement of the latter's balance of payments tends to lower, or keep low, the prevailing interest rates. This is true also if roll-over credits are lent in Euro-currencies instead of in terms of the lending country's currency.

At the time of writing the volume of roll-over credit transactions is seldom sufficiently large to produce a decisive effect on exchange rates, even if it follows a more or less uniform trend. But the possibility of the expansion of its volume should not be overlooked. It will be remembered that in the early sixties the influence of Euro-currencies – with the possible exception of Euro-dollars – on exchange rates was quite negligible, but by the end of that decade it often came to play a decisive rôle. An expansion of the roll-over credit market to an extent as to produce a similar effect is quite possible today. Even in the early Euro-currency market forward

rates came to be affected by differentials between various Euro-currency rates. An expansion of the roll-over credit market is liable to increase that effect.

The development of roll-over credits depends to some extent on the stability of exchanges. During the early seventies it must have been handicapped by the instability of exchanges which made it advisable to cover the exchange risk. During a prolonged stable period this would not be considered necessary. This would both simplify the transactions and would in given circumstances reduce the cost of the credits to the borrower or increase the yield to the lender.

A large proportion of roll-over credits is in terms of the currency of the country in which a large proportion is lent and borrowed, in which case the question of foreign exchange need not arise. Indeed it is possible to envisage a situation in which roll-over credits will become an essentially local device. History might repeat itself: acceptance credits were until the crisis of 1931 an almost entirely international device, but their local importance increased considerably before the Second World War, and even more so after the war.

Nevertheless roll-over credits are likely to remain an essentially international device. For one thing, the managing consortium usually consists of multi-national banks and/or banks of various nationalities. Also the syndicates are usually composed of lenders from a large number of countries, although this need not necessarily be the case. The raising of the funds lent to the borrowers is mostly through borrowing Euro-currencies or through buying the foreign exchange required.

But even if a roll-over credit is a purely local transac-

tion, there is nothing to prevent the borrower from spending the proceeds on imported goods or on public works contracts with foreign firms. Even such local roll-over credits are apt to lead to foreign exchange transactions. The borrower might deem it expedient to cover the exchange risk on such transactions.

The prospect of favourable interest rates is not the only consideration by which borrowers and lenders decide whether to fix the interest rate for the entire period of the credit or whether to adjust it to the market rate at fixed intervals. Variations in the rate of exchange and the premium or discount on the forward exchanges have also to be taken into consideration. On the basis of the borrower's view taken on the prospects of interest rates alone, or on Euro-dollar rates in particular if the transaction is in terms of Euro-dollars, it might appear expedient to resort to a roll-over credit. But if the borrower intends to convert the proceeds into a strong currency he would risk a loss through a devaluation of the dollar or a revaluation of the strong currency concerned, unless he covers the forward exchange, which might be a costly transaction in the circumstances. Allowing for the risk or the cost involved, the borrower might not consider it worthwhile to rely on the advantage to be gained from a decline in the interest rate of the Euro-currency concerned, especially since such a decline is often an indication of an increase in the strength of the currency of the creditor. But if the borrower takes a pessimistic view of the prospects of the lender's currency, for instance if he expects the dollar to be weak, he might find it advantageous to spend the proceeds of the credit, in spite of the likelihood of an increase in Euro-dollar

rates, since the resulting higher interest rates might be more than offset by the gain on the exchange rate. If in such situations the lender insists on lending on adjustable rates instead of fixed rates it might be worthwhile for the borrower to accept the terms offered.

CHAPTER FOURTEEN

The Official Attitude

The Euro-dollar market came into being with official blessing, and for a long time its expansion was viewed decidedly favourably in official circles. Chancellors of the Exchequer and Governors of the Bank of England quoted its remarkable growth, and the development of other parallel markets, as evidence of the vitality and inventive genius of the London banking community, which was able to maintain London's rôle as a world centre in spite of the chronic difficulties of sterling.

When towards the end of the sixties the expansion of the Euro-dollar market became self-aggravating, official circles began to be concerned about the dangers inherent in the rate of its growth and that of other parallel markets. By the time the market in roll-over credits came into being, official opinion was divided on the question of whether these developments were an unmitigated blessing, and indeed whether they were on balance a blessing at all.

Up till the time of writing no official pronouncements were uttered against the system or against its extensive use. The Bank of England likes to treat the banking community as a community of responsible adults, on the assumption that on the whole they know what they

are doing. From time to time the Bank might feel impelled to drop a gentle hint to warn this or that bank that it was going beyond the boundaries of sound and prudent banking. Warnings may be uttered to the banking community as a whole against certain practices or against their excessive use. Up to the beginning of 1973, no such general warnings were communicated to the banks concerning the misuse of roll-over credits.

This did not mean, however, that the authorities were not worried about the rate at which Euro-dollars, inter-bank deposits and CDs came to be used increasingly for financing roll-over credits. The extent of the concern with which various people in key positions in Whitehall and in Threadneedle Street viewed the situation varied widely. But there was some concern, and its extent tended to increase.

The authorities were worried, not only about the extent of the increase of the total amount of roll-over credits, but also about the quality of a high proportion of borrowers, in particular about that of borrowers on other continents. Admittedly the same borrowers – or at any rate, the same classes of borrowers – figured prominently also in the Euro-issue market. But the risk of granting roll-over credits is considered higher than the risk involved in long-term lending in the form of public issues, most of which are taken over by investors. Losses by investors would have to assume an extent comparable with the losses suffered in the Wall Street slump of 1929 and the following years before they would create an acute economic crisis. Otherwise they would merely discourage investment demand for new issues and existing stocks alike. On the other hand substantial losses by

banks on their lendings in the form of roll-over credits are apt to create a major crisis, because such losses are liable to produce chain reactions.

Even in the early thirties it was not the Wall Street slump, disastrous as it had been, that caused a series of international currency crises and banking crises. The situation did not become aggravated until the wholesale bank insolvencies of the thirties. Banks are more vulnerable than investors because, among other reasons, they lend other people's money, and they have to close their doors if they are unable to cope with the withdrawals of deposits.

The concern felt in official circles about roll-over credits did not assume the form of active discouragement. Indeed at the time of writing, early in 1973, banks were not even required to report to the Bank of England the amount of their roll-over credits as distinct from their other credits. Yet as already stated above, the authorities were concerned not only about the growing extent to which the banks had got into the habit of committing their resources for periods of five years or more, but also about the quality of their medium-term credits. Moreover it was increasingly felt that the narrowing spread did not make it possible for lenders to build up contingency reserves against bad debts. It was felt that the basic principle of the sound banking system itself was open to question. Surely it was for banks to determine interest rates instead of their allowing customers the option to gamble on changes in those rates.

Also the gradual lengthening of maturities of roll-over credits from a maximum of three years to a maximum of fourteen years caused criticism on the ground

that such long credits amounted to an evasion of statutory obligations concerning information that is required to be given to the public by borrowers who raise money through public issues. What is, after all, the difference from this point of view between a ten-year Euro-bond and a ten-year roll-over credit note?

Another point of a more technical nature is that it is supposed to be contrary to company law in England for banks to pass on liabilities (as distinct from passing on assets). Liabilities that are thus passed on unlawfully include the undertaking given by managing banks to fix the interest rate again and again for each interest period. Managing banks also give undertakings to provide participants with information about changes in the situation as and when they arise.

Many of the legal aspects of the system will have to emerge as a result of litigations. Rules will be laid down by Law Courts and by Courts of Arbitration to which the parties will submit their differences. Sooner or later legislation will be passed to regulate the activities of this new institution. Meanwhile neither the Bank of England nor the Treasury has attempted to interfere with the operation of roll-over credits.

In a sense the authorities have been actually encouraging the expansion of roll-over credits. In order to be able to operate, banks do not have to become authorised dealers, it is sufficient if they are authorised depositaries. That status can be achieved by new banks immediately after they have opened for business, long before they could become authorised dealers, which usually takes something like between three months and six months. During that interim period, the

new banks, being unable to transact business in foreign exchanges, seek to justify their existence by transacting business in roll-over credits. This is one of the contributory factors to the expansion of the volume of roll-over credits. It steps up competition, as a result of which the volume of such business increases and the quality of borrowers declines. By admitting all newcomers immediately to the status of authorised depositaries the authorities have assumed a certain amount of responsibility for developments which they themselves view with disfavour.

Of course the authorities have various means at their disposal which they could apply in order to discourage the excessive expansion of roll-over credits. The reason why the expansion gathered momentum in 1972 was because of the excessive liquidity available among the banking community brought about deliberately for the purpose of stimulating trade. Should the authorities feel too strongly about the adverse effects of the rapid expansion in roll-over credits, the remedy lies largely in their own hands. All they have to do is to create tight monetary conditions in the traditional money market and the stringency would spread over the parallel markets. Banks would be unable to supply the additional money required for the expansion of roll-over credits. By applying the credit squeeze effectively, the authorities could even reverse the unwanted trend by discouraging banks from granting new roll-over credits and from renewing expiring ones.

However strongly the authorities may feel about roll-over credits, they seem reluctant to resort to such a drastic remedy. Apart from any other reason, we have long

passed the era in which the trend of monetary policy was left in the hands of Central Banks. It has now become a matter of high politics, and the decision whether to make money fundamentally easy or tight is now reserved for the Government. The Bank of England would not be given a free hand to tighten money for the sake of restricting the expansion of roll-over credits. Since the effect of that policy might be far-reaching it is a matter for the Cabinet to decide.

There is another reason why the authorities would find it awkward to interfere with the expansion of roll-over credits, and that is because the device has greatly assisted in the provision of medium-term credit facilities; many lenders would be reluctant to commit their funds at a fixed interest rate for a period of years and, in given circumstances, borrowers would be reluctant to assume the burden of the millstone represented by high interest rates on their debts over a period of years. The system of roll-over credits has gone a long way towards enabling lenders and borrowers to overcome the difficulties of medium-term lending and borrowing. Having regard to the important part played by medium-term credits in the modern economy, the authorities would think twice before resorting to deliberate action aimed at reducing the volume of medium-term credit facilities. After all, until recently, the banking system was subject to much criticism precisely because of the lack of such facilities.

Bearing in mind what was said above, it is understandable that the authorities prefer to confine their interventions to individual instances in which the system has obviously been misused.

CHAPTER FIFTEEN

Prospects for Roll-Over Credits

Is the expansion of roll-over credits likely to continue, or is the operation of the device liable to be discontinued or at any rate greatly reduced in importance? If monetary conditions remain liquid the use of the device is likely to increase, provided that there will be no major failures which would discourage lenders. But should interest rates decline considerably it would greatly reduce demand by borrowers for roll-over credit facilities. They would prefer to borrow on fixed low interest rates. A prolonged period of cheap money – always provided that it is not expected that money would become even cheaper – would mean a prolonged decline in the demand for roll-over credits. Since, however, the banks have now acquired the know-how, it would not be difficult to revert to the extensive use of roll-over credits, if money rates should begin to rise again.

Although the monetary authorities are far from being omnipotent in determining money market conditions, they are often in a position to influence the degree of liquidity. They can thereby encourage or discourage roll-over credits. To some extent, they are therefore in a position to influence the fate of the device. They are not likely to set out to discourage its use altogether, even

though it is possible to envisage situations in which they may be anxious to call a halt to its expansion.

Sooner or later, major defaults are likely to occur. They will not necessarily undermine confidence to such an extent as to discourage lenders from granting roll-over credits altogether. It is conceivable, however, that the number or extent of the defaults might be sufficient to produce such a reaction. It seems more likely that losses by lenders or immobilisations of their assets might teach them a salutary lesson, as a result of which they would confine their operations to borrowers of a higher credit rating.

Major currency crises are liable to cause a setback in the roll-over credit market, especially if they lead to exchange controls that prevent debtors from honouring their liabilities, even if they themselves remain solvent. Wild fluctuations of exchange rates, or the expectation of such fluctuations, might discourage lenders from placing themselves in a situation in which it seems expedient to cover the exchange risk, when in fact it is too costly to do so. Exchange controls in the lenders' countries are apt to prevent them from lending, especially in terms of their own national currencies.

We saw in Chapter 10 that one of the causes of the roll-over credit boom was the spectacular increase in the number of banks. Should this expansion come to a halt or should it become reversed, there would be less incentive for banks to acquire new clients at almost any cost. The market which is now a borrowers' market might then become a lenders' market, and banks could pick and choose among applicants.

A very high proportion of roll-over credits is granted

not to the parent company, but to an affiliate. In the majority of instances, these credits are granted under the guarantee of the parent company, because the latter's credit rating is naturally higher than that of its affiliate. There is however no hard and fast rule about this matter. Credits to a multi-national borrower are not guaranteed by all its shareholders. In the absence of a contractual guarantee, a parent company might repudiate its moral obligation. This might make it difficult, if not impossible, for any affiliate ever to borrow again without a contractual guarantee from the parent company.

Prolonged liquidity would lead to a further expansion of roll-over credits and to a decline of interest rates to a level at which they would not be expected to decline further. Provided that the level of interest rates remained high because of non-stop inflation and provided that there remained a possibility of a further increase then the volume of roll-over credits would continue to expand in the absence of large-scale defaults or measures of exchange restriction or credit restriction. The market might become even more competitive, but there is a possibility that with more experience at their disposal, most lenders would become more selective.

The spread is, at the time of writing, quite unnaturally narrow, and the differentials between rates quoted for first-class borrowers and for borrowers of an inferior standing are much too narrow. Some major losses might not cause an eclipse of the market but would induce lenders to hold out for wider spreads, and differentials between rates for high-class borrowers and others would become wider.

There is ample scope for the evolution of a really good secondary market, which at present is far from adequate. A good secondary market would greatly increase the use of roll-over credits.

There is also a possibility of the development of a primary market and the possibility of a secondary market in roll-over deposits. Such deposits exist in the form of deposits to Local Authorities and have adjustable interest rates based on the rates of sterling CDs. There is no reason why this practice should not be applied more widely, and it is conceivable that deposit receipts given to lenders might develop a very active secondary market.

At the time of writing there is a complete lack of standardisation in the terms of roll-over contracts. Not only do the contracts differ widely, but even the terms are sometimes used in a different sense. Any progress towards standardisation would help to speed up negotiations, which at the moment are apt to drag on interminably. Law Court decisions or decisions by the Court of Arbitration would go some way towards clarifying the legal position, which is at present obscure in many respects.

Strangely enough no attempt has been made towards achieving some degree of standardisation. Dealers in the Eurobond market have made considerable efforts to standardise the practices in that market, and practices in markets in foreign exchange and Euro-currencies have settled down to rules which have emerged in the course of time. But the banks concerned with roll-over credits have not even formed an association or a committee to attempt to elaborate the rules. Nor is there

any exchange of information about credits other than those the terms of which are published, or between banks which have special relationships with each other. In this respect too, there is ample scope for improvement.

The institution of roll-over credits is admittedly of recent origin, but it has been in existence long enough for those actively engaged in roll-over credit transactions to realise the need for some degree of standardisation. Possibly the reasons for its complete absence lies in the keen competition between rival banking groups and in the large numbers of banks participating in many syndicates. Moreover, in a borrowers' market the borrowers have the last word. Perhaps the development of a lenders' market might pave the way towards a higher degree of standardisation, because lenders are able to determine the terms.

It would be idle to pretend that the system is perfect. Apart from the need for streamlining it, its basic principles, too, call for careful scrutiny. It may take some time before prolonged practice and more costly mistakes will bring about the improvements that are necessary in order to ensure a more flawless functioning of the system. Being a basically good system it is a pity that it is not a great deal better. It certainly deserves an effort on the part of those concerned with its functioning to bring about an improvement.

Even as it is, however, with all its flaws and defects, the roll-over credit market has been a very useful addition to the mechanism of the domestic and international monetary system. Having emerged and expanded spontaneously, without any deliberate effort on the part of

anybody to bring it into existence, it must be regarded as one of the more sophisticated monetary devices. It has yet to undergo the test of a major crisis. But even if such a crisis should bring about a setback, it would not necessarily mean that the institution would deserve to be rejected.

After all, no institution has been more misused than acceptance credits during the inter-war period, and no institution has been subjected to such severe punishment as was received by acceptance credits during the thirties. Yet acceptance credits came to be revived after the war. Those engaged in the practice have learnt their lesson, and are no longer prepared to assume the risk involved in return for a commission which was barely adequate to pay for the clerical labour involved. The institution emerged from the crisis in an improved form. It is for those engaged in roll-over credits either to learn from the experience gained in dealing with acceptance credits between the wars or to learn at their own expense and pay a comparably high price for the lesson.

Index

Acceptance credits, 15, 90, 104
Africa, 49
Amsterdam, 3

Banking centres, 2–3, 6, 93
Bank of England, 21, 93–4, 95, 96, 98
Bank rate, 12, 13
Banks:
  competition and effect on standards, 3, 51, 54–5, 72, 85–6, 97, 100, 103
  consortia of, 1, 22–3, 25
  co-operation between, 3, 25
  increase in number of, 2–3, 72, 100
  new, status of, 96–7
  participation of in secondary market, 63
  participation of in syndicates, 1, 22–4, 25, 50–1, 103
  relaxation of accepted practices by, 13, 50, 51, 72, 76–77, 96
Beirut, 3
Book credits, 1

'Borrowers' market', 25, 31, 46, 54, 100, 103
Bretton Woods Agreement, 2, 9, 11
Brussels, 3

Canada, 3, 65
Capital goods, increase in demand and production of, 4, 72, 75–6, 82–3, 85
  effect on roll-over credits, 17, 72, 75–6, 85
  inflationary effect, 81–3
Central Banks, 9, 98
Certificates of Deposits (CDs), 2, 68, 94
—, dollar, 2, 42
—, London dollar, 42, 70
—, sterling, 2, 5, 70, 102
Chancellor of the Exchequer, the, 93
Clearing banks, commercial banks, 13, 69
Coin exchange, 9–10
Communist-country borrowers, 49
Consortium credits, 22–3, 31

Index

Credit:
  exchange control, 43, 47, 62, 100
  over-lending, 85–6, 93–6
  quality of borrowers, 25, 31, 46, 47, 49, 72, 94, 95, 102
  real interest rate, 18, 74
  risks, 43, 47–51, 61–2
  squeeze, 16–17, 45, 71, 76, 77–8, 85, 97

Dalton, Hugh, 82
Depositary banks, 96–7
'Draw-down', 30, 31

Einzig, Paul: *The Case Against Floating Exchanges*, 8
Euro-bond market, vii, 2, 4, 23, 37, 42, 45, 67, 68, 102
Euro-currency markets, 2, 4, 55, 90, 102
—, effect of roll-over credits on, 87–9
Euro-dollar markets, vii, 2, 42, 58, 68, 70, 71, 84, 93, 94
— rates, 6, 31, 39, 41–2
Euro-Money, vii
Exchange control, 43, 47, 59, 62, 100
Exchange rate, fluctuations in, 9–11, 12, 44, 61–2, 100

Financing of roll-over credits:
  Euro-currencies, 90
  Euro-dollars, 70, 71, 94
  inter-bank deposits, 94
  London dollar CDs, 70, 90
  sterling CDs, 70, 90

Foreign bills of exchange, 10
Foreign exchanges, 42, 60, 102
  effect of roll-over credits on, 87–92
Forward exchanges, vii, 44, 88, 89, 91
Frankfurt, 3

Germany, 73
Gold standard, 9, 10–11

Hedging, 15, 19, 20, 42, 43, 44, 69, 74, 76, 88
Hong Kong, 3

Inflation, 13–14, 47, 71–2, 74, 76, 78–80, 81–6
  definition of, 82
  Japan, 83
  Soviet Union, 82–3
Inter-bank deposit market, 2, 4, 45, 68, 69, 70, 94
Interest rates, 11–13
—, fixed, 5, 15–16, 35–7, 45, 73
—, flexible, 3, 5, 8, 12–15, 16, 73
—, fluctuations in, 4–5, 11, 12, 13–14, 16, 43, 46–7, 53–4
—, stabilisation, role of banks in, 11–13
International Currency Review, vii
International Monetary Fund (IMF), 9, 60
International monetary system, institutional changes in, 2–5, 9–13

International note issues, 1
Iran, 49

Japan, 83
Johannesburg, 3
Jordan, 49

Keynes, Lord, 82

Latin America, 49
Lending boom in 1920s, 73
Letters of credit, 22
Liquidity, 40, 43, 44, 45–6, 67, 71–2, 97, 99, 101
Local authorities, 5, 102
London, 2, 6, 31, 60, 67, 93–4
Luxembourg, 3, 65

Managing banks, 22–4, 25, 27, 29, 30, 32, 33, 34, 37–8, 61, 64–6, 96
—, participation of in secondary market, 28, 66
Medium-term credits, 1, 3–5, 17, 44, 45, 69, 72, 73, 75–6, 98
Money markets, domestic, 31
—, international, 69, 97, 99
—, parallel, 2, 19, 93, 97
Montreal, 3
Multi-national banks, 2, 50, 90

Nassau, 3
New York, 2
Note issues, 1, 24, 25, 27

'Official mimimum lending rate', 13

Paper money, 10
Paris, 3

Roll-over credits:
    advantages, 15, 16, 17, 19–20, 45, 53–4, 76–8, 98, 103–4
    agents, role of, 27, 28, 30, 32, 33, 55, 57, 58, 65
    bearer notes, 27
    commission, 27, 30, 32
    'commitment fee', 32
    contracts: forms of, vii, 5, 21–4; negotiation of, 44–45; standardisation, lack of, viii, 5, 29–30, 102–3; terms of, 17, 22, 26, 27, 30–4, 35, 36, 37, 38–9, 40, 48, 55–7, 58, 59–61, 78, 102
    credit rating, 31, 45–6, 47, 49, 68, 72, 76, 94, 100–1
    currency: conversion during term, 59, 62; of denomination, 60; dollar option, 59–60; notice of choice, 58; options, 2, 6, 30, 32, 58–62; rate, 60; safeguards against changes in parities, 59, 61; veto of choice, 60–2
    definition, vii, 1, 3
    denomination of notes, 27, 31, 34
    depositaries, role of, 96–7
    disadvantages of, to borrowers, 18, 44–5; generally, 78

Roll-over credits – *cont.*

effect of, on developing countries, 76–7

effect of, on economic growth, 76–8

effect of, on Euro-currency markets, 87

effect of, on foreign exchanges, 88–92

executive date, 27

expansion in volume of, vii, 6–7, 68, 69–74, 76, 81, 96–97, 99, 101; causes of, 5, 14, 73

guarantees, 30, 33, 50, 101

inflationary effect of, 78–80, 81–6

interest dates, 6, 22, 32, 37, 55

— payments: currency of, 32, 59; default, 30; method of, 30; periods, 30, 32, 37, 40, 41

— rates: base rate, 22, 30, 31, 41, 42, 45, 48; limitation of upper or lower rate, 40, 53, 56; methods of adjustment, 5–6, 30, 33, 37–9, 40, 41–2; safeguards against distortion, 38–9; secondary market, 65, 67

legal aspects, 26, 31, 33–4, 48, 95–8

letters of credit, 22

managing banks, role of, 23–4, 25, 27–8, 29, 30, 32, 33, 34, 37–8, 61, 64–6

maturities, 30, 31, 52, 53; lengthening of, 5, 95–6

misuses of, 14, 46, 94–7

money brokers, 24, 37

names, limits for, 46

Participation Certificates, 23, 64

payment options, 17, 22, 27, 31, 57

Placing Memorandum, 23

Preliminary Placing Memorandum, 27

prestige value of, 25, 26, 50–51

profit margin, 41–2, 70

promissory notes, 24

prospects of, 99–104

publicisation of, 21–2, 24, 25, 26, 68, 103

reference (rate setting) banks, role of, 30, 33, 38

registered notes, 27

repayment ('drawdown'), 30, 31, 52; currency of, 32, 59; notice of, 32, 52, 55–6, 57; options, 6, 19, 30, 32, 37, 43, 52–7, 78; penalty, 32, 56–7; safeguards, changed conditions, 30, 33, 52, 54, 56, 59, 61

secondary market in, 6, 28, 37, 63–7, 102

speculation, 65

spread, 6, 22, 30, 31–2, 40, 41–2, 54, 65, 67, 70, 95, 101; definition of, 6, 41;

factors governing spread, 43–51
syndicates, 1, 22–4, 25, 27, 29, 33, 50–1, 90, 103
taxation, 30, 33
'thumbstones', 24
Roll-over deposits, 5, 102

Short-term credit, 3–4, 16–17, 75
Singapore, 3
Sinking-fund formula, 52
Smithsonian Agreement, 9
Southern Asia, 49
Soviet Union (USSR), 82–3
Spot exchanges, 88, 89
Switzerland, 3; banks, 66
Syndicated credits, 1, 3, 22–3, 25, 50–1

Tokyo, 3
Toronto, 3
Treasury, the, 96

United States of America:
banks, 3, 26, 66
participation in syndicates, 26
Regulation Q, 13
secondary market limitations, 65
Securities Act 1932, 26
Securities Exchange Commission, 26

Vienna, 3

Wall Street, 94, 95
Whitehall, 94
World Bank, 76

KU-325-589